Jeannot FATAKI N. BAZONGA

Unix/Linux operating system

Jeannot FATAKI N. BAZONGA

Unix/Linux operating system

Master Unix/Linux: From installation to system administration

ScienciaScripts

Imprint

Cover image: www.ingimage.com

This book is a translation from the original published under ISBN 978-620-6-71917-5.

Publisher:
Sciencia Scripts
is a trademark of
Dodo Books Indian Ocean Ltd. and OmniScriptum S.R.L publishing group

120 High Road, East Finchley, London, N2 9ED, United Kingdom
Str. Armeneasca 28/1, office 1, Chisinau MD-2012, Republic of Moldova, Europe
Managing Directors: Ieva Konstantinova, Victoria Ursu
info@omniscriptum.com

Printed at: see last page
ISBN: 978-620-8-57824-4

Contents

Epigraph

1. "In the world of code, where bytes dance and processes intertwine, Unix and Linux are the most agile dance partners."

2. "Where command lines cross and files intertwine are intertwined, Unix and Linux are making their way towards efficiency."

3. "Open source operating systems, such as Unix and Linux, are the foundations on which digital skyscrapers rise."

In Memoiriam

To my late Father, Papa ***Jules FATAKI MALIKIZUNGU "Julio"*** of happy memory who left us in the twilight of his life. Rest in Peace in the firmament of the Eternal God. You will remain forever engraved in our memories, we your children and also your grandchildren, great-grandchildren, ...

Born in Béni, North Kivu, on 16/06/1940 and died in Kinshasa on 15/10/2022.

"Death is no match for love.

Quote by Honoré de Balzac

"For my father. My beloved father, my own father, You who make me jump. On your knees. Like a chamois, What could I tell you. That you don't already know?"

Poem by Maurice Carême

Mama ***Henriette DISIKI NSITA***, my mother-in-law, born in Mbanza-Kongo in Kongo-Central, on 25/05/1961 and died in Kimpese in Kongo-Central on 22/12/2021. You left a great void that is difficult to fill today.

1. **To my dear mother-in-law**:

"Dear Henriette, your kindness and caring have left an indelible mark on our hearts. Your love and your smile will continue to light up our lives, even if you are gone. Rest in peace."

2. **In memory of an extraordinary woman**:

"Today we say farewell to an exceptional person. Your strength, your gentleness and your smile will remain forever engraved in our memories. May your soul rest in peace, dear Henriette DISIKI NSITA."

3. **Tribute to a mother of heart:**

"To her who was much more than a mother-in-law, but a loving mother, we express our eternal gratitude. Your legacy of love and devotion will live on in our hearts."

4. **A final farewell filled with love**:

"To her who was an infinite source of love and compassion, we say goodbye with heavy hearts. Your light will continue to shine in our lives."

Jeannot FATAKI N. BAZONGA

Dedication

To my family, colleagues, friends and everyone who contributed to this project:

Your support, encouragement and ideas were essential to the production of this book. May these pages inspire you as much as you have inspired me.

Thank you from the bottom of my heart,

Jeannot FATAKI N. BAZONGA

Acknowledgements

1. I'd like to express my gratitude to everyone who has supported me throughout this project, whether family, friends or colleagues.
2. My thanks also go to the Unix/Linux experts who shared their knowledge and experience, to the open source community for its commitment and contribution.
3. My warmest thanks go to my proofreaders and editors, who have helped to improve the quality and accuracy of this book.
4. Finally, I am grateful to my publishers and the team who worked on the publication of this book.

Preface

Dear Reader,

The author is delighted to present this book dedicated to the fascinating world of Unix and Linux. Whether you're a student, an IT professional or simply curious to learn more about these operating systems, you'll find a wealth of information here to deepen your knowledge.

The history and evolution of Unix/Linux. In the first chapter, the author goes back in time to explore the origins of Unix and Linux. From their humble beginnings in research laboratories to the ubiquitous systems you know today, you will discover how these systems have shaped modern computing. The author will also discuss the subtle differences between Unix and Linux, each of which has its own history and philosophy.

The internal structure of Unix/Linux. The second chapter delves into the internal structure of these systems. The author will examine the kernel and its functionality, as well as the file system and process management. You will understand how it all fits together to create a robust and flexible environment.

The essential commands. Navigate together with the author in the third chapter, where he explores the basic commands. From navigating the file system to manipulating processes and managing users and groups, you'll learn practical skills for working efficiently under Unix/Linux. Shell scripts, which are truly versatile tools, will also be at the heart of your discussions.

System administration in depth. The fourth chapter is dedicated to system administration. You will learn how to install Unix/Linux, configure network parameters and manage services and software packages. Security and backups will be covered in detail, because protecting your data is essential.

Programming under Unix/Linux. Finally, in the fifth chapter, the author explores programming. You will discover how to use system libraries, compile your own programs and optimise performance. Whether you are a developer or an administrator, these skills will open up new perspectives.

The author wishes you an enriching read and hopes that this book will help you on your way to mastering Unix and Linux.

Yours sincerely, Professor Doctor Engineer ***Richard KITONDUA,***

Master of the Computer Science Chair at the National Pedagogical University.

Foreword

Welcome to this book on the Unix-Linux operating system, designed to take you deep into fascinating world of these iconic operating systems. As a student with a passion for computing and networking, you are about to discover the basics and specifics of these widely used operating systems.

This book has been specially designed to help you learn and master Unix-Linux, focusing on fundamental concepts, advanced features and practical applications in the context of computer networks. You will explore in depth the architecture, resource management, security and essential tools of Unix-Linux, in order to develop a solid and relevant expertise in these crucial areas of computing.

Thanks to an interactive teaching approach, concrete examples, practical exercises and solved case studies, you will acquire essential technical skills for administering, optimising and automating system administration and network management tasks with Unix-Linux. You will also be introduced to good practice in securing systems and data, optimising performance and resolving common problems encountered in a Unix-Linux environment.

The aim of this book is to provide you with a comprehensive and practical resource to deepen your knowledge and enhance your skills in Unix-Linux operating systems, preparing you for the professional challenges you will face in the field of computer networking. Whether you want to continue your studies, develop your career or simply deepen your knowledge of computing, this book will be an invaluable guide to accompany you on your learning journey.

Thank you for your interest and commitment to learning about this crucial subject. We are confident that this book will equip you with the skills and knowledge to excel in the use and management of Unix-Linux operating systems in a network environment.

We hope that this book will be useful to you in your academic and professional career, and we encourage you to explore, experiment and deepen your skills throughout your training. We hope you enjoy reading it and discovering the exciting world of Unix-Linux!

We wish you every success in your studies and in your future professional career. May this book on the Unix-Linux operating system accompany you and help you to develop your skills and expertise in the field of computer networking. We look forward to seeing how you apply the knowledge gained from this book and to seeing you succeed in your academic and professional career.

Happy reading and learning!

Yours faithfully

The author of the book

In **Linux** and **Unix**, everything is a file. Directories are files, files are files and devices are files.

The Unix/Linux operating system plays an essential role in computer science[1]. It is widely used by IT professionals for its performance, stability and customisability. It is therefore essential to acquire a good knowledge of this operating system, particularly for Computer Science students.

Benefits of learning the Unix/Linux operating system:

1. **High demand on the job market**:

Professionals with skills in Unix/Linux are in great demand in the IT industry, offering many job opportunities.

2. **Stability and reliability**:

Unix/Linux is renowned for its stability and reliability, making it an ideal choice for mission-critical systems and demanding applications.

3. **Flexibility and customisation:**

Unix/Linux allows users to customise their working environment to suit their specific needs, offering great flexibility.

4. **Large support community:**

Unix/Linux benefits from a large community of users, which means that there are always resources available for help and advice. [1]

[1] Jean-Yvon Bimen, *Histoire de l'informatique,* Presses universitaires de France, 1992, 2e ed., 127 p. (ISBN 9782-13-044607-1).

References

1. Maurice J. Bach, "The Design of the UNIX Operating System" - Prentice Hall, 1986.
2. Brian W. Kernighan, Rob Pike, "The UNIX Programming Environment" - Prentice Hall, 1984.
3. Evi Nemeth, Garth Snyder, Trent R. Hein, Ben Whaley, "Unix and Linux System Administration Handbook" - Addison-Wesley Professional, 2017.
4. Richard Stevens, "Advanced Programming in the UNIX Environment" - Addison- Wesley Professional, 2013.
5. Mark G. Sobell, "A Practical Guide to Linux Commands, Editors, and Shell Programming" - Prentice Hall, 2017.
6. Jean-Yvon Birrien, *Histoire de l'informatique*, Presses universitaires de France, 1992, 2e ed., 127 p. (ISBN 978-2-13-044607-1).
7. Bovet, D. P., & Cesati, M. (2005). *Understanding the Linux Kernel* (3rd ed.). O'Reilly Media.
8. Russinovich, M. E., & Solomon, D. A. (2009). *Windows Internals* (5th ed.). Microsoft Press.
9. Singh, A. (2006). *Mac OS X Internals: A Systems Approach*. Addison-Wesley Professional.
10. McKusick, M. K., & Neville-Neil, G. V. (2004). *The Design and Implementation of the FreeBSD Operating System*. Addison-Wesley Professional.

A brief overview of the Unix/Linux operating system

The operating system is the heart of every computer, orchestrating the use of resources such as processors, memory, disks and peripherals.

In this book, we delve into the fascinating world Unix and Linux, two systems that have shaped modern computing.

1. Unix: The wise elder

- History: Born at Bell Laboratories in 1969, Unix was developed by Ken Thompson and Dennis Ritchie (the creator of the C language). It quickly conquered the IT world and inspired numerous variants.
- Features :

Everything is a file: Unix considers everything (including peripherals) to be files.

Time-sharing multitasking: Several programs run simultaneously.

Multi-users: Several people can work on the same system.

Shell as a command interpreter: The Shell allows you to interact with the system.

Configuration stored as text: easy to manage.

Available on various hardware architectures: from PCs to supercomputers.

Used in universities, research centres and Internet servers.

2. Linux: The free heir

- History: In 1991, Linus Torvalds, a Finnish student, created the Linux kernel. Thousands of contributors took part in its development.
- Free software: Linux is open source, code available on the Internet.
- Linux distributions: Each distribution (Ubuntu, Fedora, etc.) adds installation and administration to the Linux kernel.

May this exploration of Unix and Linux systems inspire you in your writing.

Chapter 1

Introduction to Unix/Linux

1.1 History and development of the Unix/Linux operating system

The genesis of Unix

Un PDP-7
A PDP-7

In 1969, Ken Thompson and Dennis Ritchie, then working for Bell Laboratories, developed the first version of a single-user operating system under the name *New Ken's System*. They did this on a DEC PDP-7 (*Programmed Data Processor*) minicomputer running the General Comprehensive Operating System and wrote the new software in assembly language. The name Unics was suggested by Brian Kernighan following a 'Latin' pun on Multics; "Multi-car Multics did the same thing in several ways, whereas Unics did everything in one way". The name was later contracted to Unix (and eventually registered as UNIX by AT&T), on Brian Kernighan's initiative.

A consent decree dating from 1956 prohibited AT&T, the company to which Bell Labs belonged, from marketing anything other than telephone or telegraph equipment. This is why the decision was taken in 1975 to distribute the complete Unix system with its source code to universities for educational purposes, in return a licence at a very low price.

In 1971, aware of the difficulty maintaining a system written in assembly language, Ken Thompson considered rewriting Unix in TMG, but found that TMG did not offer what he needed. For a short time he considered rewriting Unix in Fortran, but finally designed B with the help of Dennis Ritchie in 1969 and 1970, based on the BCPL language. However, Unix was never rewritten in B; B did not support types, all variables were the same size as the words in the architecture, arithmetic on floats was not implemented and the B compiler used threaded code. So in 1971 Dennis Ritchie set about writing *New B*, which was renamed C. C is still one of the most widely used languages today.

Ken Thompson and Dennis Ritchie presented the first paper on Unix at the Symposium on Operating Systems Principles at Purdue University in 1973. Professor Bob Fabry of the University of California Berkeley (UCB), then in the

audience, was immediately interested and in January 1974 Keith Standiford, a student, installed *Version 4* at UCB, distributed on magnetic tape.
In early 1975, Ken Thompson spent a year as a visiting professor at his *alma mater*, UBC. Together with Jeff Schriebman and Bob Kridle, they set up *Version 6*, which was when Unix began to be distributed outside Bell Labs.

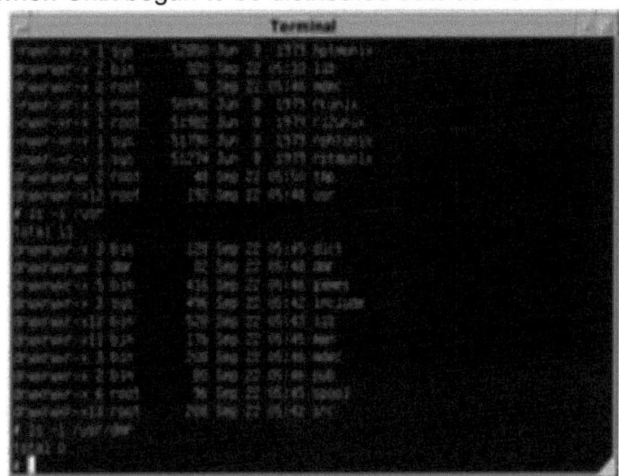

Unix version 7 on a PDP-11 emulator

In the autumn of 1975, Bill Joy and Chuck Haley, then in their second year, became interested in the new system and implemented the *ex-line* editor in Pascal, eventually exploring how the kernel worked when Ken Thompson left. Alan Snyder, Steven C. Johnson and Michael Lesk between 1973 and 1977. At the beginning of the latter year, Bill Joy produced the first *Berkeley Software* Distribution (BSD). Later, with the arrival of new terminals, he wrote vi (the visual editor), an overlay *for ex*. In the summer of 1978, the *Second Berkeley Software Distribution* or 2BSD was born.

At the same time, the concepts of datagrams and distributed computing were emerging, with Arpanet, the Cyclades network and the Distributed System Architecture, which became the OSI-DSA model in 1978. More communications between machines in different research centres demonstrated the usefulness of open and convergent operating systems, which would become a necessity with the first workstations including TCP/IP from Sun Microsystems, created by Andy Bechtolsheim, Bill Joy, Vinod Khosla and Scott McNealy.

Then in December 1979, Bill Joy distributed 3BSD, the first distribution to support DEC VAX computers. This was also the year that version 7 was released, with a number of notable changes, such as extending the maximum file size to 2 GB, adding several utilities and, above all, making the system more *portable*, meaning that it was easier to modify so that it could run on other hardware platforms. It was at this time that the first major port of Unix, version 32/V, was produced, on a VAX 11/780.

Expansion

At the end of 1977, researchers at the University of California made numerous improvements to the Unix system supplied by AT&T and distributed it under the name Berkeley Software Distribution (or BSD). BSD was, for example, the first

Unix system to make full use of the VAX 11/780 paged virtual memory mechanism.

Three main branches of springs development came into being:

- AT&T's research branch, which developed the 8th, $9^{(th)}$ and $10^{(th)}$ editions of the Unix system at Bell Laboratories until 1990.
- The commercial arm of AT&T, which developed System III, then four editions of System V (System V, SVR2, SVR3, SVR4).
- Berkeley Software Distribution developed by the University of California at Berkeley until 1994.

These branches have borrowed code and/or concepts from each other. Thus :

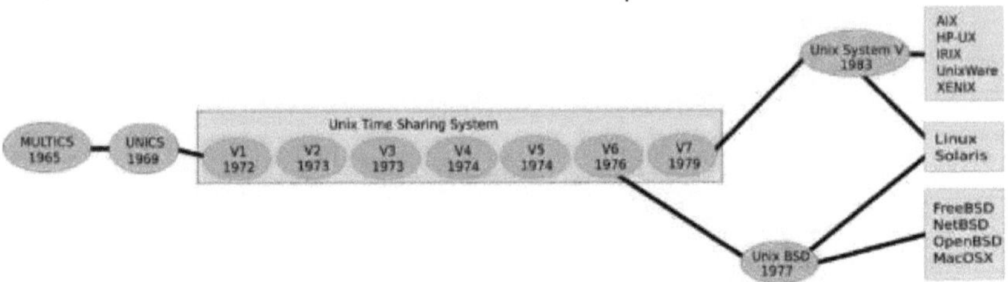

Chronology and parentage of the various Unix and related systems.

- The 8th edition is based on BSD version 4.1.
- The SVR3 version has borrowed the concept of standard flows from the 8th edition.
- The SVR4 version incorporates a lot of code from BSD version 4.3.
- Version 4.4 BSD contains a very small amount of code from the SVR4 version.

Uses of Unix

There are a large number of variants of Unix, each with its own specific features, enabling Unix systems to be used in a large number of different environments.

Mobile devices

Several operating systems for mobile devices (smartphones, tablets, PDAs, etc.) are Unix systems. These include iOS and Android, which share over 85% of the smartphone market.

Supercomputers

Since November 2017, Linux has been the only operating system used by the world's 5o0 most powerful supercomputers. Other Unix systems still equipped some of these computers in 2016. Between 1995 and 2000, Unix systems other than Linux (including Berkeley Software Distribution, Solaris, AIX, UNICOS and HP-UX) equipped more than 90% of these computers.

Workstations and servers

Only a few versions of Unix produced by major workstation and server manufacturers remain today:

. IBM : AIX ;

- Oracle : Solaris ;
- Hewlett-Packard : HP-UX ;
- SCO Group: UnixWare

The philosophy of Unix workstation and server manufacturers was initially to develop an operating system to sell their machines, adding, if possible, a little 'extra' to set them apart from the competition. This was forgetting that most Unix systems are heterogeneous and that any difference from one machine to another, even when created with the best intentions in the world, threatens interoperability and therefore constitutes a real risk of counter-productivity, as it forces IT specialists to carry out numerous tedious operations in order to interconnect the systems.

This is one of the reasons why many of these manufacturers now offer the GNU/Linux system with their servers. However, the differences between the various Linux distributions often pose the same problems, albeit to a lesser degree.

Some computer-aided design software has long been available for Unix workstations only, but as this market shrinks, it has also become available for other systems. This is the case, for example, with CATIA, used in particular by major industrial manufacturers such as Dassault Aviation, PSA Peugeot Citroên and Boeing, which has been running on Microsoft Windows since version 5, while the Unix version has been discontinued since version 6.

1.2. Key features and benefits.

What is Unix?

Unix is one of **the oldest operating systems**. Since its creation, it has developed into a large family of operating systems with many variants. There are free open source offshoots as well as proprietary variants, most of which have been officially licensed by the Open Group and are available for a fee[2] . Today, Unix is mainly installed on **servers and, in particular, on high-performance workstations**. The main features of this operating system are :

- open source until the 1980s, then proprietary ;
- open source offshoots are also available (e.g. FreeBSD);
- one of the first operating systems based on the C programming language;
- independent of any hardware platform and processor type (C-based Unix code is portable and can be flexibly adjusted to the hardware environment concerned);
- multitasking (several programs or processes can easily be run in parallel);
- multi-user system (several users can work on the same system, and data and resources can be blocked or shared for access by other users);
- adapted to multiprocessor systems ;
- the central kernel of the operating system manages system and process activities; non-kernel software is organised into separate processes;
- hierarchical file system (now standard, this was an innovation when it was introduced in 1980);
- secure (there are few Unix-based malicious programs; Unix has good rights management, encryption technologies and remote access via Secure Shell) ;
- network-compatible (TCP/IP integrated), extensive network functionality (e.g. Unix network tools), full range of services as a network server ;

[2] Maurice J. Bach, "The Design of the UNIX Operating System" - Prentice Hall, 1986.

- complete basic equipment (including essential development and libraries) ;
- professional programming concepts, automated by advanced scripting ;
- increased system stability, for example through memory protection;
- a standardised programming interface (POSIX).

Note;

POSIX (Portable Operating System Interface) defines a **standardised programming interface** enabling operational collaboration on application software with the Unix operating system. IEEE and Open Group are the leaders in the development of POSIX. POSIX forms the basis of the Single UNIX Specification. A Unix operating system that complies with the Single UNIX specification can use the UNIX trademark (UNIX in capitals, sometimes supplemented by the Registered Trademark® symbol). There are Unix offshoots and derivatives that are fully compatible (e.g. IBM's AIX) or largely compatible (e.g. Linux) with POSIX.

Unix family (outline)	Branches / derivatives
AT&T UNIX derivatives/System V line	AIX (IBM; certified as UNIX 98 and 03)
	HP-UX (Hewlett Packard; certified as UNIX 95 and 03)
	Oracle Solaris (Oracle; certified as UNIX 95, 98, 03 and V7)
BSD range (BSD = Berkeley Software Distribution)	FreeBSD (there are different distributions and different derivatives)
	NetBSD (there are different distributions and different derivatives)
	OpenBSD (there are different distributions and different derivatives)

What is Linux?

Linux is an operating system **available free of charge** on the Internet and developed by a worldwide open source community. However, there are also closed source projects, mainly in the commercial sector. Like Unix, Linux has also spawned numerous offshoots (known as "Linux distributions and derivatives" = derivatives of a Linux distribution) that extend the operating system kernel and make it an operating system in its own right. **Linux distributions** are often developed for a specific application. For example, there are desktop systems and specific operating systems for servers.

Linux is often likened to Unix or referred to as a **Unix-like operating system**, particularly because it was designed as a Unix-like system, includes typical Unix features and many Linux applications also run on Unix. However, Linux does not contain **any proprietary Unix code**, nor is it currently verified by the Open Group as an official UNIX system.

The main features of Linux are :

- open source ;
- open system development by a worldwide community of developers ;
- mostly free, with a few commercial versions available for a fee;
- Linux distributions complement the Linux kernel with practical and application-oriented software ;

- adapted to multiprocessor systems ;
- multitasking (several programmes running in parallel) ;
- multi-user systems ;
- supports a wide range of CPUs and hardware platforms (desktop PCs, supercomputers and mainframe computers, servers);
- suitable for small mobile and electronic devices (routers, home automation devices, Internet of Things) ;
- Linux is in largelywrittenin C (the programs in C programsa high portability between different operating systems and computers);
- wide selection of software and user interfaces ;
- comprehensive security features (encryption technologies, sophisticated system and rights management, Secure Shell for secure remote access);
- sophisticated scripting (e.g. programming and automation using Shell scripts) ;
- standardised interfaces (POSIX, Linux Standard Base/LSB).

Note

The **Linux Standard Base (LSB)** defines the main **standards** (e.g. for binary interfaces and program libraries) to optimise compatibility between different Linux distributions.

Popular Linux distributions and	**Special features**
Debian	Distribution with a wide choice of software, supports 12 processor architectures
Ubuntu	Debian derivative optimised for home computers
Linux Mint	An offshoot of Ubuntu designed for beginners, with a range of desktop environments
Knoppix	First popular live distribution (portable, no installation required), wide range of software, derived from Debian
Gentoo	Source-based Linux distribution for advanced users, the system can be fully customised
Red Hat Enterprise Linux (RHEL)	Well-known Linux server distribution for businesses (currently market leader), full support thanks to independent software manufacturers, chargeable, part of the Fedora project
Fedora	The direct successor to Red Hat Linux (RHL), specialising in server and desktop systems, in many cases replaces RHL whose development has been discontinued, and is also designed for beginners.
openSUSE	Complete Linux distribution, particularly popular in Germany and the United States, uses the RPM package manager (free package management system), own configuration tool (YaST)

1.3. Differences between Unix and Linux

Comparison of Linux and Unix properties and functions

Comparing Unix and Linux, there are **many similarities**. Both systems are multi-user, allow multitasking and guarantee high system stability thanks to RAM protection. IT professionals and system administrators can use sophisticated scripts and a command prompt to control and program. The two systems also offer **mutual compatibility thanks to the POSIX specification**. In particular, this enables utilities to be exchanged seamlessly, and greatly simplifies cross-system migrations and porting.

Usually, work in **client/server architectures** can be done quickly and efficiently with Unix. Nor does the number of utilities available leave anything to be desired for IT professionals and experienced system administrators. And if they don't find what they're looking for, they can **program their own application**. Today, Linux users can use equally sophisticated systems that are continually being optimised and equipped with modern features thanks to the dynamic development of the open source community.

In terms **of software**, the two systems stand out for their complete basic equipment with utilities and basic software. The Linux distributions also offer an integrated, user-friendly **package manager**. Via the Internet, this manager accesses the software directory with current and tested programs. A "package maintainer" maintains the program packages in an update directory, which contains both free and paid-for programs. In addition, compared with Unix, Linux offers a greater variety of operating systems and user interfaces (e.g. the KDE and Gnome desktop environments), particularly for normal desktop users.

Unix and Linux security

Security is a key issue when comparing Unix and Linux. Both are considered to **be particularly secure operating systems**. The specific architecture of the system makes it much more difficult to cause fundamental damage. Authorisations and access rights can be handled in a highly differentiated and detailed way, and **user management** allows users to be clearly separated. In a multi-user system, each user has their own data space to which no other user has unauthorised access. This prevents any loss of data due to accidental deletion. In addition, users do not have access to important system files. Unix and Linux allow secure remote access via Secure Shell (SSH). Virtually all Unix- and Linux-based operating systems offer a pre-configured SSH program.

Another advantage shared by the Linux and Unix systems is that the number of **viruses and malware targeting these OSes is insignificant**. The low prevalence of these OSes on desktop PCs has a positive impact here, since hackers generally specialise in exploiting security flaws in particularly widespread software and hardware (e.g. Windows programs). However, it is now becoming clear that Linux systems, in particular, are **increasingly being targeted by hackers** due to their growing prevalence on servers, routers and Internet of Things devices. As a result, security vulnerabilities in the Linux kernel need to be regularly patched. In addition, Unix and Linux servers can spread malware to Windows PCs in the network.

Comparing the use of Linux and Unix

For many years, there was **no uniform user interface** for classic versions of Unix. However, since the mid-1980s, the X Window System has allowed various utilities to be equipped a GUI (graphical user interface) that can be used with the mouse and keyboard. However, because of the different implementations and the disparity of graphical interfaces between different applications, we **cannot speak of a uniform, cross-application graphical user interface concept**. Current Unix systems can use intuitive desktop environments such as KDE and Gnome.

These and other IGUs are also available for Linux. As far as possible, the developer community is aiming to make Linux a universal solution **for virtually all** available **platforms**, and is also targeting wider target groups with a greater diversity easily accessible user interfaces. For the Gnome desktop environment, for example, there is a user interface that allows **Linux to** be used **in much the same way as Windows 10**.

For both these OSes (but mainly for Unix), use via a terminal and a command prompt (terminal concept) is widespread. This is partly due to the fact that, particularly in the server domain, many administrative tasks can be carried out and automated **more economically with a shell** (even between computers on the network). The standard shell for using the command prompt is called Bash on most Linux systems. Many Unix systems use the Bourne shell.

Unix vs Linux: advantages and disadvantages

Advantages of Unix	Advantages of Linux
Stable, sophisticated environment mainly for servers and workstations.	A versatile OS, particularly well suited to the server market (server-specific Linux distributions are available), many Clouds use Linux.
Works on a wide range of hardware platforms (portability),	Extensive, manufacturer-independent hardware support (applies to CPUs
tailor-made solutions for optimum adjustment to the equipment.	servers, workstations, PCs, minicomputers).
Pay-per-use UNIX systems are continually being developed to meet customer requirements.	Most distributions are free (cD/DVD, Internet download).
Secure (e.g. restriction of user rights, encryption).	Secure (e.g. restriction of user rights, encryption).
Sophisticated scripting (Shell).	Sophisticated scripting (Shell).
Ideal for programmers and system administrators.	Ideally suited to programmers and system administrators, more intuitive IGUs especially for desktop users.
Wide choice of programs and tools (many of which are already included in the OS).	Wide choice of programs and tools (many of which are already included in the OS).
Particularly suited to critical business areas.	With frequent updates, security flaws are quickly corrected.
Thanks to the POSIX standard, Unix applications can also run on Linux (migration possible).	Thanks to the POSIX standard, Linux applications can also run on Unix (migration possible).
	Low hardware requirements, good

	system performance.
	Portable versions without installation available (e.g. on DVD, USB stick).
Disadvantages of Unix	**Disadvantages of Linux**
Limited target group, focusing on experienced users and IT professionals.	Beginners Linux will need a certain amount of time to adapt , and new users will have to give up some of their usual software.
Many (specific) solutions on the server market are chargeable and linked to a specific manufacturer's hardware.	On the server market, higher support costs may apply if commercial Linux distributions are used.
Hardware requirements are usually higher (particularly in the case of commercial licence-based systems).	Linux security flaws and malicious programs (servers are particularly at risk).
Rather infrequent updates and slow development.	Drivers for new hardware (PCs, graphics cards) are published after a certain period of time.
The number of users is falling, partly because of Linux (particularly in the server market).	Trend towards fragmentation in Linux development (large number of Linux distributions).
Virtually insignificant on the desktop market.	Low market share for desktops and laptops.

Linux vs Unix: a comparison of these operating systems

The history and development of Unix[3]

If we compare Unix and Linux directly, we can certainly call Unix a pioneer in computing. The broad outlines of this OS (OS = operating system) were developed **in the 1960s** by employees of Bell Labs (whose parent company was AT&T). Following publication of the source code for the initial version (dating from 1969), a large number of offshoots and successors were created in the years that followed. As a result of this ramified and uncoordinated development, there is no such thing today as "one Unix", but rather a vast Unix universe or Unix family. Within this Unix family, two main lines have set the tone for many years: **BSD and System V**.

The **Berkeley Software Distribution** (BSD for short) was created in 1977 at the University of California, Berkeley, as a variant of the Unix operating system. Over time, the initial version gave rise to a complete family tree of Unix derivatives. Among the best-known distributions are FreeBSD, OpenBSD and NetBSD, from which other BSD projects have been developed. BSD-licensed Unix software **can be used freely**. For licensing reasons, FreeBSD no longer includes any original Unix code from the AT&T line.

The **System V family** is the second main development branch that has produced the UNIX systems from IBM (AIX), Hewlett Packard (HP-uX) and Oracle (Oracle Solaris), which are still in commercial use today. When it was introduced in 1983,

[3] Brian W. Kernighan, Rob Pike, "The UNIX Programming Environment" - Prentice Hall, 1984.

System V was initially used to refer only to a derivative Unix in particular. Today, it is used to designate a whole family or class of Unix derivatives **derived directly from the AT&T UNIX line**, and generally under official licence.
The boundaries between these two families of Unix system development **are fluid and often overlap**. At present, these two main branches are moving ever closer together, as technical innovations from one branch are often taken up by the competing line. In practice, it also happens that an operating system with BSD components is officially UNIX-certified by the Open Group (macOS BSD code, but since version Leopard 10.5 has also had official UNIX 03 certification).

The age and development of Linux

Linux is the most recent player in our Linux vs Unix comparison. This unixoid operating system was released in 1991 by its developer **Linus Thorvalds**. Strictly speaking, at that time the Finn had only made available a **modular operating system (the Linux kernel)** which functioned as a single central interface for a wide range of hardware and was used to manage memory and processes, as well as multitasking and security functions.
The Linux kernel was then shared with the **open source community** in 1992 under the **GPL free licence**. The licensing kick-started a worldwide development that has spawned various **Linux distributions** and derivatives. A distribution, for example, completes the Linux kernel to form a fully-fledged operating system with a compiler, libraries and interfaces for user interaction. However, lite versions of Linux, which operate very much at hardware level on small devices for example, only require a relatively small amount of additional software.
The **GNU project** is one of the most influential communities of Linux developers. The GNU/LHUX distributions are widely used in desktop and server systems. It is crucial for the dynamic development of distributions and derivatives that the Linux universe is not subject to restrictive licences, licence costs and lengthy licensing procedures. Linux was first developed for **Intels x86 hardware processors**. Today, it is available for more than twenty types of CPU. Linux is also compatible with ARM processors for mobile devices and small appliances (smartphones, tablets, media players, mini-computers such as the Raspberry Pi and various handheld devices).

Unix: distribution, costs and target groups

Initially, Unix was mainly used **in universities and on specific workstations**. The operating system then increasingly used on servers and in computer centres. Today, Unix suppliers concentrate on paying customers, mainly from the free enterprise and industrial sectors (e.g. financial services providers, large industrial groups and customers from the healthcare sector). Today, if someone wants to use Unix professionally on servers or workstations, they generally have to buy **verified, licensed proprietary UNIX versions** from manufacturers such IBM (AIX), Oracle (Oracle Solaris) or Hewlett Packard (HP-UX). These manufacturers offer a complete package with perfectly matched hardware and software, so Unix often runs on PA-R|SC and Itanium machines. Licence fees vary according to the extent of the complete server hardware package required and the number of software licences.
Customers in the industrial and business sectors particularly value **stability and**

security and prefer to use AT&T's proprietary UNIX systems in business-critical areas. In this segment, Unix systems will continue to play a role, as large companies often have **long-term licensing, support and maintenance contracts** Unix suppliers. In addition, moving from a complete, customised Unix system to another system architecture can be quite costly and involves technical risks.

On the whole, however, the popularity and spread of Unix **has been declining for some time**, partly as a result of technical development. Modern Windows and Linux systems have traditionally run on x86 processor architectures, which are relatively inexpensive and currently in the majority. They are evolving rapidly and now dominate the standard server market. By contrast, traditional server systems (e.g. Itanium machines with UNIX systems from the System V family) **are not currently making as much technical progress** and are not cost-effective solutions.

Having been adapted from the outset for very specific areas of application and experienced users (IT professionals, programmers, system administrators), Unix systems **usually play little part in** the mass market for laptops and desktops. However, despite the decline in its use and its focus on business-critical areas, Unix's current influence should not be underestimated. In our Unix vs. Linux comparison, BSD systems score particularly well in terms of distribution. Apple's macOS uses Unix code; free Unix derivatives such as FreeBSD are among the most widely used operating systems in the world beyond the desktop and laptop markets. FreeBSD is increasingly used for mail servers, web servers, firewalls, FTP servers and DNS servers. It is also installed on routers and NAS hardware.

Linux: distribution, costs and target groups

Because of its advantages, which are hard to ignore, **Linux is becoming increasingly popular**. Linux is characterised by broad hardware support, open source, free access (CD, DVD, Internet download), free of charge even for multiple installations, rapid development and good scalability, as well as optimum adaptability to hardware and application environments and specific requirement profiles. What's more, **POSIX compatibility** makes it easy to migrate from older Unix systems. is also helping to spread Linux.

Linux is currently most **popular in the server sector**. It is estimated that at least half of all servers run on Linux operating systems. There are also paid versions specifically for the server market (Red Hat Enterprise Linux), which offer better **customer support but are also more expensive**. Linux is also widespread in the mobile phone sector. Google's popular Android operating system is a distribution with a modified Linux kernel. Smaller devices (e.g. telephones, minicomputers, routers) often use lighter versions of Linux (embedded Linux systems).

When it comes to desktops, Linux plays a secondary role, even though it has been the third most popular PC operating system in the world since 2009. But this position should not mislead us, because in July 2020, its market share of page views worldwide was just 1.9% (data collected on the basis of Internet use with desktops and laptops, smartphones and tablets are not included).

Even so, it's true that the low-cost **desktop** version of **Linux has managed to**

establish itself in certain niches (e.g. government institutions and organisations). On the whole, however, Linux is still seen as the preferred solution for hobbyists, ambitious PC users and IT professionals who, for example, want to be independent of US companies and are also able to use a command prompt. Clearly, many users are reluctant to give up Windows or MacOS. It seems that many of them **do not want to invest in a new operating system** and switch to new user programs.

Linux vs Windows: operating systems put to the test

Most PC users have only ever known Windows in its successive versions. But there are alternatives on the operating system market. Linux distributions offer many advantages over Microsoft's product. But you need to think carefully before deciding to change your operating system.

Chapter 2

Structure of the Unix/Linux operating system

2.1. Kernel and its functions

The Linux® kernel is the main component of a Linux operating system and is the interface between a computer's hardware and its processes. It ensures communication between the two and manages resources as efficiently as possible.

What functions does the kernel of an operating system have?

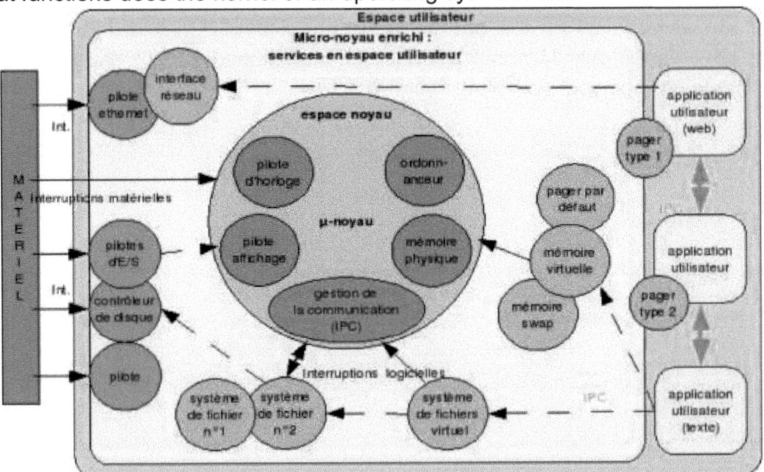

Architecture of a microkernel enriched by services (enriched microkernel)

An operating system kernel is one of the fundamental parts of some operating systems. It manages the computer's resources and enables the various components - hardware and software - to communicate with each other.

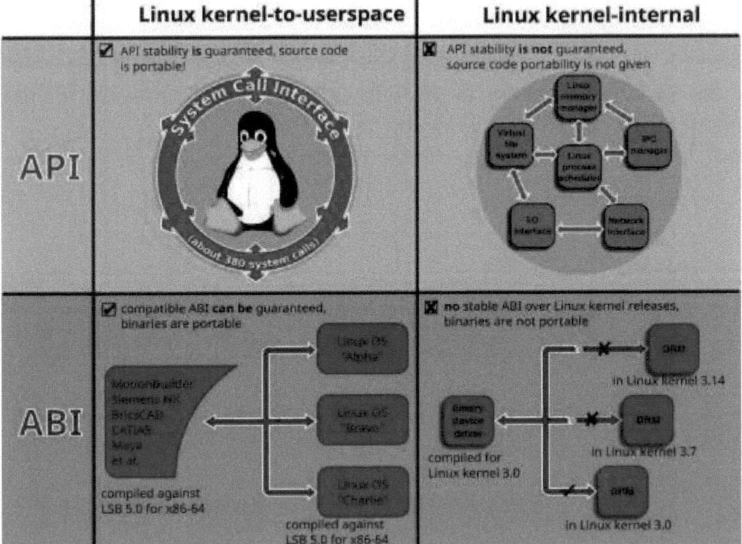

Its main characteristics are that it is multitasking and multi-user. It complies with POSIX standards, making it a worthy heir to the UNIX systems. Initially, the kernel was designed to be monolithic. This technical choice was the subject of heated debates between Andrew S. Tanenbaum, a professor at the Free University of Amsterdam who had developed minix, and Linus Torvalds.

This famous debate between Andrew S. Tanenbaum and Linus Torvalds concerns the design of operating system kernels. Tanenbaum, creator of Minix, argued that modern kernels should be microkernels, because of their modularity and stability. On the other hand, Torvalds, the creator of Linux, argued that microkernels did not offer good performance compared with monolithic[4] kernels.

This discussion took place in the 1990s and had a significant influence on the development of operating systems. The Linux kernel, although monolithic, became modular, allowing features to be added or removed on the fly.

2.2. File system and process management

What is a file system?

A file system is a **system of classification and organisation on a storage medium** that structures and organises the writing, searching, reading, storing, modifying and deleting of files in a specific way. It is important that files can be identified without error thanks to their classification and that users can **access their files as quickly as possible.** File systems also define parameters such as the following:

- File naming conventions
- File attributes
- Access control(s)

File systems are also an important operational component, acting as an interface

[4] http s ://www. wikiwand. com/en/Noy au_L inux

between the operating system and all connected drives (internal and external, via a USB port for example).
File systems are **formatted** on a data medium, and the storage media purchased today are already formatted. In the past, it was common practice for users to prepare new data media for storing and managing files.

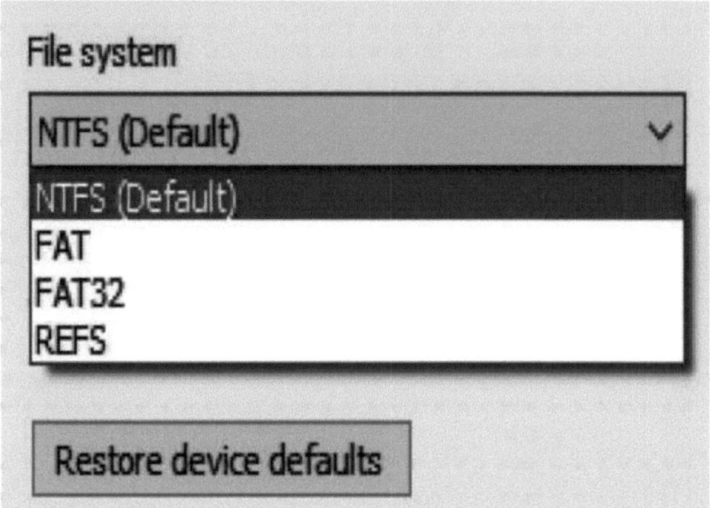

Formatting options, including selection of the file system for an external data medium (NTFS format is standard in recent versions of Windows).

Overview of the main file systems

There are **various standard file systems** for Windows, macOS, Linux, Unix & Co. In recent years, differentiation has increased due to technical advances, for example customised file systems have been developed for the increasingly popular flash memory media (USB sticks, SSD drives). What all file systems have in common is that they use a tree structure for organisation, starting with the root directory. From there, folders or directories and sub-folders branch out.

note:

Despite certain similarities, file systems **are generally not compatible with each other**. For example, if you connect a mobile hard drive with APFS (Apple File System since 2017) to a Windows computer, you won't be able to make it work. What's more, the file systems used under Linux are not directly supported in support by other systems operating systems. In rule

In general, however, there are solutions in which, for example, **special software from third-party suppliers** read and write access to a data medium.

There are a number of file systems available today, but **not all of them are widely used**. Currently, the most common systems are FAT16, FAT32, exFAT and NTFS (Windows) as well as HFS+ and APFS (macOS/Mac OS X). Linux currently uses ext4 (successor to ext3 and ext2) among others. The file systems mentioned are briefly presented below.

FAT (File Allocation Table)

The file system has been around since 1980 and the variants published since then are known as "FAT12", "FAT16" and "FAT32". FAT formatting is ideal for managing and **exchanging small amounts of data**. Today, however, the FAT file system is actually outdated, because even in its most recent and powerful variant (FAT32, introduced in 1997), files can have a maximum size of 4 gigabytes (GB). FAT32 also limits the maximum partition size to 8 terabytes (TB).

Despite these limitations, FAT formats are still very common. They are used for **mobile removable media** (external hard drives, USB sticks) and specific hardware (digital cameras, smartphones, routers, televisions, car radios, etc.). They are synonymous with the highest possible compatibility, especially in the field of mobile telephony.

exFAT (Extended File Allocation Table)

The 2006 format is an evolution of the classic FAT format. exFAT was originally designed for removable media and is therefore particularly suited to USB sticks, memory cards and external hard drives such as solid state drives (SSDs) with individual storage capacities. exFAT works particularly well with **rather small data storage devices.** However, it can also handle large files and easily **exceeds the 4GB limit** set by FAT32. Since Windows 7, exFAT has been natively supported (it is present as a standard tool, without installation of any additional driver or special service pack).

NTFS (New Technology File System)

The NTFS file system was introduced in 1993 with the Windows NT operating system. Since Windows Vista, it has been the standard file system for Windows computers. It offers a number of advantages over FAT, such as the ability **to compress data media** and **to enhance data security** (e.g. through encryption). A special feature of NTFS is that access and file and folder sharing can be defined in detail and exhaustively. Users can assign rights for local and remote access via the network.

HFS+ (Hierarchical File System)

The file system was introduced by Apple in 1998 as a complementary development to HFS. To clearly distinguish the two standards, they are also referred to as Mac OS Extended (HFS+) and Mac OS Standard (HFS). Compared with HFS, HFS+ is faster and more efficient at managing, reading and writing data. It can also manage more files, with up to 4 billion blocks of files or folders. Linux can partly read and write directly to disks with HFS+, but specific packages may need to be installed (hfsutils, hfsplus, hfsprogs). On Windows, additional software is required for full HFS+ support.

APFS (Apple File System)

APFS, which was developed by Apple in 2017, **meets the needs of modern SSDs in particular**. APFS is designed as a 64-bit system, with data and file encryption also possible. If an operating system is based on an SSD, the file system is automatically converted from HFS+ to APFS. This "auto-formatting" was introduced with the High Sierra operating system. Since Mac OS 10.14 Mojave, Fusion drives (logical drives formed from SSDs and mechanical hard drives) are also automatically converted to APFS. When converting from HFS+ to APFS, however, problems can sometimes occur.

ext4

ext4 was launched in 2008 as the successor to station 3. The file system is currently standard on many Linux systems (e.g. Ubuntu). The most important innovation is the Extents function, which optimises the management of large files and prevents fragmentation more effectively than its predecessors. Under ext4, partitions can be resized at will while the system is running. The maximum size of the file system was limited to 32TB for ext3, but for ext4 it is much higher: 1 exabyte (approximately 1 million Terabytes).

Summary table: the main file systems

Name	Applications	Operating systems	Features
FAT32	Mobile data media	- Windows - Mac OS X/macOS - Linux (install drivers if necessary)	- high compatibility - extensive hardware support - no encryption or compression functions - Data security is not particularly emphasised - ideal for small scores - maximum file size: 4 GB
exFAT	Mobile data media	- Windows - Mac OS X/macOS (Compatible from 10.6.4) - Linux (install drivers if necessary)	- not yet a common standard. - no rights management - no data compression - ideal for small flash memories from 32 GB (USB sticks, SD cards) - unlimited sizes and partitions (according to current state of the art) - maximum file size: 512 terabytes
NTFS	Internal and external hard drives	- Windows - Mac OS X/macOS (full complete only with an additional tool) - Linux (after driver installation)	- legal administration - improved data security: protection against data loss and modification, possibility of data encryption - Data can be compressed,
			high performance with large data carriers - specialised for large files and large storage capacities - not suitable for small disks and partitions of less than 400 MB (too much management effort)

			- maximum file size: 256 TB
APFS	SSD drives	- macOS (Standard from version 10.13, High Sierra) - Software for use with older Mac OS and Windows operating systems	- optimised for Solid State Drives (SSDs) and other flash storage devices - is also working on mechanical and hybrid discs - data encryption possible - optimised memory management (space-sharing function) - The fault protection function protects against damage to the file system (e.g. in the event of a system failure). - MacOS support for Fusion Drive 10.14 Mojave - maximum file size: 8 Exbibyte
HFS+	Internal and external hard drives	Mac OS X/macOS	- an advanced, proven file system - particularly suitable for mechanical discs - not optimised for modern storage technologies (SSD, Flash)
			- better backward compatibility than APFS - limited lifespan, unlikely to be supported by Apple in the long term - will lose more and more importance as a result of the partially automated "forced conversioninto the APFS - maximum file size: 8 Exbibyte
ext4	Linux	- Linux - Windows (only with a tool additional) - Mac OS X/macOS (only with an additional tool)	Compared to previous Ext versions : - improved performance - improved data security - integrated encryption (from Linux kernel 4.1) - the new Extents function offers advantages in terms of speed for managing large files

			and prevents fragmentation - rights management possible - maximum file size: 16 TB

Changing file systems: is it possible?

Compatibility is very important when choosing a format, for example if you want to use an external hard drive not only locally on your PC, but also across multiple platforms and devices. For maximum flexibility when transferring data between an Apple device and a Windows device, for example, we recommend formatting with the exFAT file system. **The right choice when it comes to formatting** a data medium is therefore of great importance, and can avoid problems and restrictions in the day-to-day exchange data .[5]
However, if the basic conditions are met (for example, the current hardware), the system can also be replaced at any time, for example to switch from an old file system to a **more modern** one. However, it is essential to determine beforehand whether a change can be made without **losing files and data**, or whether all the data must first be backed up and then copied to the new data medium[6] . There are both free and paid programs for these transfers that make the process safer and more convenient. However, this can also be done in part using the built-in resources of an operating system. In our article "Formatting a USB stick", you can find out, for example, how to change the file system on a USB stick directly in Windows.

System process management commands

The following table describes the commands for managing system processes.

Table Process management commands

Ordering	Description	Manual page
ps, pgrep, prstat, pkill	Checks the status active processes on a system and displays detailed information on the process.	ps(1), pgrep(1) andprstat(1M)
Pkill	Works exactly like pgrep but searches for or flags processes by name or some other attribute and terminates the process. Each matching process is reported as with the kill command, rather than having its process ID printed.	pgrep(1), and pkill(1) kill(1)
pargs, preap	Facilitates process debugging.	pargs(1) and preap(1)
dispadmin	Lists the default process planning strategies.	dispadmin(1M)
Priocntl	Assigns processes to a priority class and manages the priorities of the	priocntl(1)

[5] https://www.commentcamarche.net/informatique/stockage/1425-choisir-un-systeme-de-fichiers-pour-le-formatting/
[6] Bovet, D. P., & Cesati, M. (2005). *Understanding the Linux Kernel* (3rd ed.). O'Reilly Media.

	process.
Nice	Changes the priority of a nice(1) time-sharing process.
Psrset	Binds processing groups to a psrset(1M) group of processors rather than a single processor.

The Processes tool in the Solaris Management Console lets you manage processes using a user-friendly interface.

Using the ps command

The ps command allows you to check the status of active processes on a system and display technical information about the processes. This data is useful for administrative tasks such as determining process priorities.

Depending on the options used, the ps command displays the following information:

- Current status of the process
- Process ID
- Parent process ID
- User ID ;
- Programming class
- Priority
- Process address
- Memory used
- CPU time used

The following table describes some of the fields indicated by the ps command. The fields displayed depend on the option chosen.

Table: Summary of ps report fields

Field	Description
UID	Effective user ID of the process owner.
PID	Process ID.
PPID	ID of the parent process.
C	Use of the processor for programming purposes. This field is not displayed when the -c option is used.
CLS	Programming class to which the process belongs, such as real-time, system or time-sharing. This field is only included with the -c option.
PRI	Programming priority of the kernel thread. A higher number indicates a higher priority.
NI	Nice number of the process, which contributes to its programming priority. Making a process more pleasant is equivalent to lowering its priority.
ADDR	Address of the proc.
SZ	Process virtual address size.
WCHAN	Address of an event or lock for which the process is on standby.
STIME	Process start time in hours, minutes and seconds.
TTY	Terminal from which the process, or its parent, was started. A question mark indicates that there is no control terminal.
TIME	Total amount of CPU time used by the process since it was started.
CMD	Command that generated the process.

Using the file system and /proc commands

You can view detailed information about the processes listed in the /proc directory using process commands. The following table lists /proc process commands. The /proc directory is also known as the process file system (PROCFS). Images of active processes are stored here according to the process ID number.

Table: Process commands (/proc)

Ordering the process	Description
Pcred	Displays process identification information.
Pfiles	Indicates the fstat and fcntl information relating to the files opened in a process.
Pflags	Prints monitoring indicators /proc, waiting and pending signals, and other status .
Pldd	Lists the dynamic libraries linked to a process.
Pmap	Prints the address space configuration for each process.
Psi	Lists the signal actions and managers for each process.
Plum	Starts each process.
Pstack	Prints a hex+symbolic stack trace for each lwp in each process.
Pstop	Stops each process.
Ptime	Accounts for the time taken by a process using microstate accounting.
Ptree	Displays the process trees containing the process.
Pwait	Displays status information once a process has finished.
Pwdx	Displays the current working directory of a process.

For more information, see proc(1).

Process tools are similar to some ps command options, except that the output provided by these commands is more detailed.

a general rule, process commands perform the following operations:

- Display more information about processes, such as the fstat and fcntl directories, working directories and parent and child process trees.
- Control processes by authorising users to stop or resume them.

Process management with process commands (/proc)

You can display detailed technical information about processes or control active processes using certain process commands. See the Table for a list of some /proc commands.

If a process is trapped in an infinite loop or is taking too long to run, you can stop the process using the kill or pkill command, see Managing system processes (tasks).

The /proc file system is a directory hierarchy containing additional sub-directories for status information and control functions.

The /proc file system also provides an xwatchpoint function which is used to reconfigure read/write permissions on the various pages of a process's address . This function has no restrictions and is MT-safe.

The debugging tools have modified to use the xwatchpoint function in /proc, which means that the whole xwatchpoint process is faster.

The following restrictions have removed when you define xwatchpoints using the dbx debugging tool:

- Definition of xwatchpoints on local stack variables due to registry windows on the SPARC system.
- Definition of xwatchpoints on multithreaded processes.

For more information, see the details on proc and mdb.

List of processes

- **Use the `ps` command to list all the processes on a system.**

```
$ ps [-efc]
```

ps

Displays only the processes associated with your connection session.

-ef

Displays complete information about all processes running on the system.

-c

Displays information about the process scheduler.

Example 1 Process list

The following example illustrates the output of the ps command when no options are used.

```
$ ps
  PID TTY      TIME COMD
  1664 pts/4   0:06 csh
  2081 pts/4   0:00 ps
```

The following example illustrates the output of the ps - ef command. This output indicates that the first process executed when the system initializes is sched (the swapper), followed by init, pageout, and so on.

```
$ ps -ef
     UID   PID  PPID  C    STIME TTY      TIME CMD
    root     0     0  0   Dec 20 ?        0:17 sched
    root     1     0  0   Dec 20 ?        0:00 /etc/init -
    root     2     0  0   Dec 20 ?        0:00 pageout
    root     3     0  0   Dec 20 ?        4:20 fsflush
    root   374   367  0   Dec 20 ?        0:00 /usr/lib/saf/ttymon
    root   367     1  0   Dec 20 ?        0:00 /usr/lib/saf/sac -t 300
    root   126     1  0   Dec 20 ?        0:00 /usr/sbin/rpcbind
    root    54     1  0   Dec 20 ?        0:00 /usr/lib/sysevent/syseventd
    root    59     1  0   Dec 20 ?        0:00 /usr/lib/picl/picld
    root   178     1  0   Dec 20 ?        0:03 /usr/lib/autofs/automountd
    root   129     1  0   Dec 20 ?        0:00 /usr/sbin/keyserv
    root   213     1  0   Dec 20 ?        0:00 /usr/lib/lpsched
    root   154     1  0   Dec 20 ?        0:00 /usr/sbin/inetd -s
    root   139     1  0   Dec 20 ?        0:00 /usr/lib/netsvc/yp/ypbind ...
    root   191     1  0   Dec 20 ?        0:00 /usr/sbin/syslogd
    root   208     1  0   Dec 20 ?        0:02 /usr/sbin/nscd
    root   193     1  0   Dec 20 ?        0:00 /usr/sbin/cron
    root   174     1  0   Dec 20 ?        0:00 /usr/lib/nfs/lockd
  daemon   175     1  0   Dec 20 ?        0:00 /usr/lib/nfs/statd
    root   376     1  0   Dec 20 ?        0:00 /usr/lib/ssh/sshd
    root   226     1  0   Dec 20 ?        0:00 /usr/lib/power/powerd
    root   315     1  0   Dec 20 ?        0:00 /usr/lib/nfs/mountd
    root   237     1  0   Dec 20 ?        0:00 /usr/lib/utmpd
       .
       .
       .
```

Process information display

1. **Obtain the ID of the process for which you want to view more information.**

```
# pgrep process
```

where *process* is the name of the process for which you want to display more information.

The process ID is displayed in the first column of the output.

2. **Display the process information you need.**

```
# /usr/bin/pcommand pid
```

pcommand

Represents the command (`/proc`) to be executed. Table 12-3 lists and describes these commands.

pid

Identifies the process ID.

Example 2 Displaying process information

The following example illustrates how process commands can be used to display more information about a `cron` process.

```
# pgrep cron 1
4780
# pwdx 4780 2
4780:    /var/spool/cron/atjobs
# ptree 4780 3
4780  /usr/sbin/cron
# pfiles 4780 4
4780:    /usr/sbin/cron
  Current rlimit: 256 file descriptors
   0: S_IFCHR mode:0666 dev:290,0 ino:6815752 uid:0 gid:3 rdev:13,2
      O_RDONLY|O_LARGEFILE
      /devices/pseudo/mm@0:null
   1: S_IFREG mode:0600 dev:32,128 ino:42054 uid:0 gid:0 size:9771
      O_WRONLY|O_APPEND|O_CREAT|O_LARGEFILE
      /var/cron/log
   2: S_IFREG mode:0600 dev:32,128 ino:42054 uid:0 gid:0 size:9771
      O_WRONLY|O_APPEND|O_CREAT|O_LARGEFILE
      /var/cron/log
   3: S_IFIFO mode:0600 dev:32,128 ino:42049 uid:0 gid:0 size:0
      O_RDWR|O_LARGEFILE
      /etc/cron.d/FIFO
   4: S_IFIFO mode:0000 dev:293,0 ino:4630 uid:0 gid:0 size:0
      O_RDWR|O_NONBLOCK
   5: S_IFIFO mode:0000 dev:293,0 ino:4630 uid:0 gid:0 size:0
      O_RDWR
```

1. Gets the `cron` process ID.
2. Displays the current working directory of the `cron` process.
3. Displays the process tree containing the `cron` process.
4. Displays `fstat` and `fcntl` information.

Process control

1. **Obtain the ID of the process to be controlled.**

```
# pgrep process
```

pgrep *process*

where *process* is the name of the process to be controlled.

The process ID appears in the first column of the output.

2. **Use the appropriate process command to control the process.**

```
# /usr/bin/pcommand pid
```

/usr/bin/pcommand pid

pcommand

Represents the process command (`/proc`) to be executed.

This document lists and describes these commands.

pid

Identifies the process ID.

3. **Check the status of the process.**

```
# ps -ef | grep pid
```

ps -ef | grep *pid*

Example 3 Process control

The following example shows how to use the process command to stop and restart the `dtpad` process.

```
# pgrep dtpad 1
2921
# pstop 29212
# prun 2921 3
```

1. Gets the ID of the `dtpad` process.
2. Stops the `dtpad` process.
3. Restarts the `dtpad` process.

Stopping a process (`pkill, kill`)

It is sometimes necessary to stop (interrupt) a process. The process may be in an infinite loop. Or you may have started a large job that you want to stop it is finished. You can interrupt a process that you own. A superuser can interrupt any process on the system except processes with IDs `0`, `1`, `2`, `3` and `4`. Interrupting these processes may cause the system to crash.

For more information, `see the pgrep`(1), `pkill`(1) and `kill`(1) manual pages.

End of process (`pkill`)

1. (Optional) **To terminate another user's process, log on as a superuser (or equivalent role).**
2. **Obtain the ID of the process to be terminated.**

```
$ pgrep process
```

where *process* is the name of the process to be terminated.

Example:

```
$ pgrep netscape
587
566
```

The process ID is displayed in the output.

Note - To obtain more information about a Sun Ray process, use the following commands :

```
# ps -fu user
```

This command lists all user processes.

```
# ps -fu user | grep process
```

This command searches for a specific process for a user.

3. **End the process.**

```
$ pkill [signal] process
```

When no signal is included in the `pkill` command line syntax, the default signal used is -15 (`SIGKILL`). Using the -9 (`SIGTERM`) signal with the `pkill` command ensures that the process is terminated as quickly as possible. However, the -9 signal should not be used to stop certain processes, for example a database or LDAP server process. This could result in the loss of data.

process

Represents the name of the process to be stopped.

Tip - When you use the `pkill` command to interrupt a process, use the command itself first, without including a signal option. Wait a few minutes to see if the process finishes before using the `pkill` command with the -9 signal.

4. **Check that the process has been interrupted.**

```
$ pgrep process
```

The interrupted process must no longer appear in the output of the `pgrep` command.

End of process (`kill`)

1. (Optional) **To terminate another user's process, log on as a superuser (or equivalent role).**
2. **Obtain the ID of the process to be stopped.**

```
$ ps -fu user
```

where *user* is the user whose processes you wish to display.

The process ID is displayed in the first column of the output.

3. **End the process.**

```
$ kill [signal-number] pid
```

signal

When no signal is included in the `kill` command line syntax, the default signal used is -15 (`SIGKILL`). Using the -9 (`SIGTERM`) signal with the `kill` command ensures that the process is terminated as as possible. However, the -9 signal should not be used to stop certain processes, for example a database or LDAP server process. This could result in the loss of data.

pid

Represents the ID of the process to be stopped.

Tip - When you use the `kill` command to stop a process, use the command itself first, without including a signal option. Wait a few minutes to see if the process finishes before using the `kill` command with the -9 signal.

4. **Check that the process has been interrupted.**

```
$ pgrep pid
```

The interrupted process must no longer appear in the output of the `pgrep` command.

Debugging a process (pargs, preap)

The `pargs` and `preap` commands improve process debugging. The `pargs` command prints out the arguments and environment variables associated with a live process or kernel file. The `preap` command deletes dead (zombie) processes. A zombie process has not yet had its exit state claimed by its parent. These processes are generally harmless but can consume system resources if there are many of them[7] . You can use the `pargs` and `preap` commands to examine the processes whose privileges you want to check. As a superuser, you can examine processes.

Example 4 Debugging a process (pargs)

The `pargs` command solves a long-standing problem related to the impossibility of using the `ps command` to display all the arguments passed to a process. The following example shows how to use the `pargs` command with the `pgrep` command to display the arguments passed to a process.

```
# pargs `pgrep ttymon`
579:    /usr/lib/saf/ttymon -g -h -p system-name console login:
-T sun -d /dev/console -l
argv[0]: /usr/lib/saf/ttymon
argv[1]: -g
argv[2]: -h
argv[3]: -p
argv[4]: system-name console login:
argv[5]: -T
argv[6]: sun
argv[7]: -d
argv[8]: /dev/console
argv[9]: -l
argv[10]: console
argv[11]: -m
argv[12]: ldterm,ttcompat
548:    /usr/lib/saf/ttymon
argv[0]: /usr/lib/saf/ttymon
```

The following example shows how to use the pargs - e command to display the environment variables associated with a process.

```
$ pargs -e 6763
6763: tcsh
envp[0]: DISPLAY=:0.0
```

2.3 Managing users and permissions

User and rights management (task list)

In Trusted Extensions, you take on the role of security administrator to administer users, permissions, rights and roles. The list of tasks below describes common tasks you perform for users working in a tagged environment.

Task	Description	See

7
Russinovich, M. E., & Solomon, D. A. (2009). *Windows Internals* (5th ed.). Microsoft Press.

Modifying a user's label range	Modifies the labels under which a user can work. Modifications can limit or extend the range authorised by the label_encodings file.	Modifying a range of user labels
Creating a rights profile for convenient authorisations	There are several authorisations that can be useful for standard users. Creates a profile for users considered suitable for these authorisations.	Creating a rights profile for convenient authorisations
Changing the game a user's default privileges	Deletes a privilege from the privilege set using user default.	Limitation of user privileges
Deactivation of the account locking for individual users	Locking users' accounts that can take on a role must be deactivated.	Deactivation of the account locking for certain users
Grant of authorisation to modify the data label on a user	Authorises a user to upgrade or downgrade information.	Granting of authorisation modify a user's data security level

Complete deletion of a user and its processes Deletion of a user from the system.process user account

Trusted Extensions system

Modifying a range of user labels

You may wish to extend a user's label range to give them read permissions to an administration application. For example, a user authorised to connect to the global zone can then view the list of systems running on a particular label. The user can view the content but not modify it.

You may also wish to restrict the user's label range. For example, a guest user may be limited to one label.

Before you start

You must be a security administrator in the global zone.

- Do one of the following:

- **To extend the user's label range, assign a higher-level authorisation.**

```
# usermod -K min_label=INTERNAL -K clearance=ADMIN_HIGH jdoe
```

You can also extend the user's label range by reducing minimum label.

```
# usermod -K min_label=PUBLIC -K clearance=INTERNAL jdoe
```

o **To limit the label range to a single label, the authorisation must be equal to the minimum label.**

```
# usermod -K min_label=INTERNAL -K clearance=INTERNAL jdoe
```

Creating a rights profile for convenient authorisations

Where permitted by the site security policy, you may wish to create a rights profile containing permissions for users who are authorised to perform tasks requiring authorisation[8] . To enable all users on a particular system to be authorised, see Changing policy.conf defaults.

Before you start

You must be a security administrator in the global zone.

1. **Create a rights profile containing one or more of the following permissions.**

The following authorisations may be useful for users :

o solaris.device.allocate: authorises a user to allocate a device, such a microphone or CD-ROM.

By default, Oracle Solaris users can read and write to a CDROM. However, in Trusted Extensions, only users who can allocate a device can access the CD-ROM drive. Disk allocation requires authorisation. Therefore, to read and write to a CD-ROM in Trusted Extensions, a user needs Allocate Device permission.

o solaris.label.file.downgrade: authorises a user to downgrade the security level of a file.

o solaris.label.file.upgrade: authorises a user to increase the security level of a file.

o solaris.label.win.downgrade: authorises a user to select information from a higher-level file and place it in a lower-level file.

o solaris.label.win.noview: authorises a user to move information without viewing the moved information.

o solaris.label.win.upgrade: authorises a user to select information from a lower-level file and place it in a higher-level file.

o solaris.login.remote: authorises a user to connect remotely.

o solaris.print.nobanner: authorises a user to print on paper without a cover page.

o solaris.print.unlabeled: authorises a user to print on paper without a label.

o solaris.system.shutdown: authorises a user to shut down the system and stop a zone.

2. **Assign the rights profile to a user or role.**

For a step-by-step procedure, see Modifying a User's Security Attributes in the Oracle Solaris 11.1 Administration: Security Services manual.

Limiting a user's privilege set

Site security may require that users have fewer privileges than they are assigned by default. For example, on a site that uses Trusted Extensions on Sun Ray systems, you may want to prevent users from viewing other users' processes on

[8] Evi Nemeth, Garth Snyder, Trent R. Hein, Ben Whaley, "Unix and Linux System Administration Handbook" - Addison-Wesley Professional, 2017.

the Sun Ray server.

Before you start

You must be a security administrator in the global zone.

- **Remove one or more privileges in the `basic` game.**

Warning - Do not delete the `proc_fork` or `proc_exec` privilege. Without these privileges, a user cannot use the system.

```
# usermod -K defaultpriv=basic,!proc_info,!proc_session,!file_link_any
```

By removing the `proc_info` privilege, you prevent the user from examining processes that do not originate from the user. Removing the `proc_session` privilege prevents the user from examining processes outside their current session. By removing the `file_link_any` privilege, you prevent the user from creating physical links to files that do not belong to the user.

Deactivation of the account lock for certain users

Carry out this procedure for all users who can take on a role.

Before you start

You must be a security administrator in the global zone.

- **Disable account locking for a local user.**

```
# usermod -K lock_after_retries=no jdoe
```

To disable account locking for an LDAP user, specify the LDAP repository.

```
# usermod -S ldap -K lock_after_retries=no jdoe
```

Granting authorisation to a user to modify the data security level

A standard user or role can be authorised to modify the security level or labels of selected files, directories or texts. The user or the role, in addition to having authorisation, must be configured to be able to work on more than one label. In addition, tagged areas must be configured to allow their tags to be modified .[9]

Warning - Changing the data security level is a privileged operation. This task can only be performed by trusted users.

Before you start

You must be a security administrator in the global zone.

- Assign the Object Label Management rights profile to the appropriate users and roles.

Example 5 Authorising a user to upgrade the label of a file without being able to downgrade it

The Object Label Management rights profile allows users to upgrade or downgrade labels. In this example, the administrator allows a trusted user to upgrade but not downgrade data.

The administrator creates a rights profile based on the Object Label Management profile and removes the Downgrade File Label and Downgrade DragNDrop or

[9] https://www.ibm.com/docs/fr/devops-release/7.0.0?topic=security-roles-permissions

CutPaste Info permissions from the new[10] profile.

```
# profiles -p "Object Label Management"
profiles:Object Label Management> set name="Object Upgrade"
profiles:Object Upgrade> info auths
...
profiles:Object Upgrade> remove auths="solaris.label.file.downgrade,
solaris.label.win.downgrade"
profiles:Object Upgrade> commit
profiles:Object Upgrade> end
```

The administrator then assigns the profile to a trusted user.

```
# usermod -P +"Object Upgrade" jdoe
```

Deleting a user account from a Trusted Extensions system

When a user is deleted from the system, you must ensure that the user's home directory and all objects belonging to the user are also deleted. As an alternative to deleting objects belonging to the user, you can transfer ownership of these objects to a valid user.

You must also ensure that all batch processes associated with the user are also deleted. No objects or processes belonging to a deleted user can remain on the system.

Before you start

You must be a system administrator in the global zone.

1. **Archive the user's home directory under each label.**
2. **Archive the user's mail files under each label.**
3. **Delete the user account.**

```
# userdel -r jdoe
```

4. **In each tagged zone, manually delete the user's directories and mail files.**

Note - You are responsible for finding and deleting temporary user files under all labels, such as files in /tmp directories.

[10] Singh, A. (2006). *Mac OS X Internals: A Systems Approach*. Addison-Wesley Professional.

Chapter 3

Basic Unix/Linux commands

3.1 Browsing and manipulating files and directories

To navigate Linux files and directories, use the cd command. Depending on your current working directory, this command requires either the full path or the directory name. Running this command without any options will take you to your home folder.

Here are the 40 most popular basic Linux commands you should know:

Most people think that Linux is a complicated operating system that is only used by **programmers**. But learning Linux isn't as scary as it sounds. You don't need to take a **programming course** or master a programming language. In this short but comprehensive chapter you will discover **the basic Linux commands** and how to use them like a pro.

Linux is an entire family of **open-source** Unix operating systems based on the Linux kernel.

This includes all the most popular Linux-based systems such as Ubuntu, Fedora, Mint, Debian and others. More precisely, they are called distributions or distros.

Since it was first published in **1991**, Linux has continued to grow in popularity because of its open-source nature. People can freely modify it and redistribute it under their own name.

When you use a Linux operating system, you need to use a shell - an interface that gives you access to system services. Most Linux distributions use a graphical user interface (GUI) as a shell, mainly to make it easier for users to use.

That said, it is recommended that you use a **command line interface (CLI)** because it is more powerful and more efficient. By typing text commands, you can perform tasks that require a multi-step process via the GUI, in just a few seconds.

So if you are planning use the Linux operating system, learning the **basic commands** will be very useful. In this chapter, you will learn **40 basic Linux commands** that will undoubtedly help you navigate Linux as a beginner.

What is a Linux command?

A Linux command is a program or utility that runs on the command line (CLI) - a console that interacts with the system through text and processes. It is similar to Windows Command Prompt application.

Linux commands are executed on the terminal by pressing Enter at the end of the line. You can run commands to perform a variety of tasks, from installing packages to managing users and manipulating files.

This is what general syntax of a Linux command looks like:

Command name [option(s)] [parameter(s)].

A command can contain an **option** or a **parameter**. In some , it can be executed without them. These are the three most common parts of a command

Command name: this is the rule you want to run.

Option or flag: modifies the operation of the command. To invoke it, use dashes (-) or double dashes (-).

Parameter or argument: specifies any information required by the command. Remember that all Linux commands are case-sensitive.

The 40 most frequently used Linux commands

Before moving on to the list of basic commands, you must first open Terminal. If you're still unsure, have a look at the **tutorial on the command line**.

Although the steps may differ depending on your Linux distribution, the Terminal application is generally found in the **Utilities** section.

Here is the list of basic Linux commands:

1. sudo command

Short for superuser do**, sudo** is one of Linux's most popular basic commands, allowing you to perform tasks requiring administrative or **superuser** permissions. When sudo is used, the system asks users to authenticate themselves with a password. The Linux system then records a timestamp as a trace. By default, each root user can run sudo commands for **15 minutes/session**.

If you try to run sudo from the command line without authenticating, the system will log the activity as a security event.

Here is the general syntax:

sudo (command)

You can also add an option, for example :

- **k** or **-reset-timestamp** invalidates the timestamp file.
- **g** or **-group=group** executes commands as the specified group name or ID.
- **h** or **-host=host** executes commands on the host.

2. pwd command

Use the **pwd** command to find the path to your current working directory. Simply entering **pwd** will give you the full path, i.e. the path to all directories starting with a slash (**/**). For example, **/home/username**.

The **pwd** command uses the following syntax:

pwd [option]

It has 2 possible options:

-L or **-logic** displays the contents of environment variables, including symbolic links.

-P or **-physical** displays the actual path of the current directory.

3. Order cd

To navigate Linux files and directories, use the command **cd.** Depending on your current working directory, this command requires either the full path or the directory name.

Running this command without any options will take you to the home folder. Bear in mind that only users with **sudo** privileges can run it.

Suppose you are in the **/home/username/Documents directory** and want to access **Photos**, a subdirectory of **Documents**. To do this, enter the following command:

cd Photos.

If you want to change to a completely new directory, for example **/home/username/movies**, you need to type **cd** followed by the absolute path of the directory:

cd /home/username/ films

Here are a few shortcuts to help you navigate:

cd ~[username] allows access to another user's home directory.

cd ... mount a directory.
cd- returns you to the previous directory.

4. ls command

The **ls** command lists the files and directories on a system. If run without flags or parameters, this command displays the contents of the current working directory. To display the contents other directories, type **ls** followed by the desired path. For example, to display the files in the **Documents** folder, enter :

ls /home/username/Documents

Here are some options you can use with the **ls** command:

ls -R lists all the files contained in the subdirectories.
ls -a displays hidden files in addition to visible files.
ls -lh displays file sizes in easy-to-read formats such as MB, GB and TB.

5. Order cat

Concatenate, or **cat**, is one of the most frequently used Linux commands. It enumerates, combines and writes the contents of files to standard output. To run the cat command, type **cat** followed by the name of the file and its extension. For example :

cat filename.txt.

Here are some other ways of using the **cat command**:

cat > filename.txt creates a new file.
cat filename1.txt filename2.txt >
filename3.txt merges **filename1**.txt and **filename2.txt** and stores the result in **filename3.txt**.
tac filename.txt displays the contents in reverse order.

6. Order cp

The **cp** command is used to copy files or directories and their contents. Take a look at the following use cases.

To copy a file from the current directory to another, enter **cp** followed by the name of the file and the destination directory. For example :

cp filename.txt /home/username/Documents

To copy files to a directory, enter the file names followed by the destination directory :

cp filename1.txt filename2.txt filename3.txt
/home/username/Documents

To copy the contents of a file to a new file in the same directory, enter **cp** followed by the source and destination files:

cp filename1.txt filename2.txt

To copy an entire directory, pass the **-R** option before typing the source directory, followed by the destination directory :

cp -R /home/username/Documents /home/username/Documents_backup

7. Command mv

The mv command is mainly used to move and rename files and directories. It does not produce any results at runtime.

Simply type **mv** followed by the name of the file and the destination directory. For example, you want to move **filename.txt** to the **/home/username/Documents** directory:

mv filename.txt /home/username/Documents.

You can also use the **mv** command to rename a file:

mv old_file_name.txt new_file_name.txt

8. mkdir command

The **mkdir** command can be used to create one or more directories at a time and set the permissions for each of them. The user executing this command must have the right to create a new folder in the parent directory, otherwise they receive a "permission denied" error message.

Here is the basic syntax:

mkdir [option] directory_name

For example, you want to create a directory called **Music** :

mkdir Music

To create a new directory called **Songs** inside Music, use the following command:

mkdir Music/Songs

The **mkdir** command accepts many options, such as :

- **p** or **-parents** create a directory between two existing folders. For example, **mkdir -p Music/2024/Songs** will create the new directory "2024".
- **m** file access rights. For example, to create a directory with permissions full of read write and execution for all the users, enter **mkdir -m777 directory_name**.
- **v** displays a message for each directory created.

9. rmdir command

To permanently delete an empty directory, use the **rmdir command**. Remember that the user executing this command must have **sudo** privileges in the parent directory.

For example, you want to delete an empty subdirectory called **personal1** and its main folder **mydir** :

rmdir -p mydir/personal1

10. rm command

The **rm** command is used to delete files in a directory. Make sure that the user running this command has write permissions.

Don't forget the directory location, as this operation will delete the file(s) and you won't be able to undo it.

Here is the general syntax:

rm filename

To delete several files, enter the following command:

rm filename1 filename2 filename3

Here are some acceptable options you can add:

- **i** asks the system to confirm the deletion of a file.
- **f** allows the system to delete without confirmation.
- **r** deletes files and directories recursively.

11. Touch control

The **touch command** is used to create an empty file or to generate and modify a timestamp from the command line.

For example, enter the following command to create an HTML file named **web** in the **Documents** directory:

touch /home/username/Documents/web.html

12. Order locate

The **locate command** is used to find a file in the database system.

In addition, adding the **-i** argument disables case , allowing you to search for a file even if you don't remember its exact name.

To search for content containing two or more words, use an asterisk (*). For example, the asterisk (*) is used search for content containing two or words:

locate -i school*note

The command searches for files containing the words **school** and **note**, whether in upper or lower case.

13. Order find

The **find** command is used to search for files in a specific directory and perform the following operations. Here is the general syntax:

find [option] [path] [expression]

For example, you want to search for a file called **notes.txt** in the **home** directory and its subfolders :

find /home -name notes.txt

Here are some other ways of using **find** :

find -name filename.txt to search for files in the current directory.

find ./ -type d -directory name to search for directories.

14. grep command

Another basic command on the list is **grep** or **global printing of regular expressions**. It allows you to find a word by browsing all the text in a specific file. When it finds a match, this command displays all the lines containing the specific word. This command can also be used to filter large log files.

For example, you want to search for the word **blue** in the file **notepad.txt :**

grep blue notepad.txt

The output of the command will display the lines containing **blue**.

15. df command

The **df command** is used to find out how much disk space the system using, as a percentage and in kilobytes (KB). Here is the general syntax:

df [options] [file]

For example, enter the following command if you want to see the disk space usage of the current directory in a human-readable format:

df -h

Here are some acceptable options to use:

df -m displays information on file system usage in **MB**.

df -k displays file system usage in **KB**.

df -T displays the file system **type** in a new column.

16. Ordering the

If you want to check the space occupied by a file or directory, use the **du** command. You can run this command to identify the part of the system that is using storage space excessively.

Remember that you must specify the path to the directory when you use the **du** command. **For example**, to check **/home/user/Documents**, enter :

from /home/user/Documents

Adding a flag to the **from** command modifies the operation, for example :

- **s** shows the total size of a specified folder.
- **m** provides information on folders and files in **MB**

k displays information in **KB**.

- **h** informs you when the folders and files displayed were last modified.

17. Order head

The **head** command displays the first ten lines of a text. By adding an option, you can change the number of lines displayed. The **head** command is also used to send data to the command line.

Here is the general syntax:

head [option] [file]

For example, you want to display the first ten lines of the file **note.txt**, located in the current directory :

headnote.txt

Below are some options you can add:

- **n** or **-lines** displays the first custom number of lines. For example, enter **head -n 5 filename.txt** to display the first five lines of **filename.txt**.
- **c** or **-bytes** displays the first custom number of bytes in each file.
- **q** or **-quiet** does not print the headers specifying the file name.

18. Order tail

The **tail command** displays the last ten lines a file. It allows users to check whether a file contains new data or to read error messages.

Here is the general format:

tail [option] [file]

For example, you want to display the last ten lines of the **colors.txt** file**:**

tail -n colors.txt

19. Order diff

Short for difference, the **diff** command compares two contents of a file line by line. After analysing them, it displays the parts that do not match.

Programmers often use the **diff** command to modify a program instead of rewriting all the source code.

Here is the general format:

diff [option] file1 file2

For example, you want to compare two text files - **note.txt** and **note_update.txt** :

diff note.txt note_update.txt

Here are some acceptable options to add:

- **c** displays the difference between two files in a contextual form.
- **u** displays the output without the redundant information.
- **i** makes the **diff** command case insensitive.

20. Order tar

The **tar command** allows you archive several files in a **TAR** file **-** a common Linux format similar to **ZIP**, with optional compression.

Here is the basic syntax:

tar [options] [archive_file] [file or directory to archive]

For example, you want to create a new **TAR** archive named **newarchive.tar** in

the **/home/user/Documents** directory:
tar -cvf newarchive.tar /home/user/Documents
The **tar** command accepts many options, such as :

- **-x** extracts a file.
- **-t** lists the contents of a file.
- **-u** archive and adds to an existing archive file.

See the **practical examples** to find out more about the other functions.

21. Command chmod

chmod is a common command that changes the read, write and execute permissions of a file or directory. Under Linux, each file is associated with three classes of user: **owner**, **member of a group** and **others**.

Here is the basic syntax:
chmod [option] [permission] [filename]
For example, the owner is currently the only user with full permissions to modify **note.txt**. To allow members of the group and other people to read, write and execute the file, assign it the **-rwxrwxrwx** authorisation type, with a numeric value of **777** :
chmod 777 note.txt
This command has a number of options, including

- **-c** or **-changes** displays information when a modification is made.
- **-f** or **-silent** suppresses error messages.
- **-v** or **-verbose** displays a diagnostic for each file processed.

22. Command chown

The chown command lets you change the ownership of a file, directory or symbolic link to a specific user name.

This is the basic format:
chown [option] owner[:group] file(s)
For example, you want to make **linuxuser2** the owner of **filename.txt** :
chown linuxuser2 filename.txt

23. Job order

A job is a process that the command launches. The **jobs** command displays all the processes currently running and their status. Remember that that this command is only available in the **csh**, **bash**, **tcsh** and **ksh** shells.

This is the basic syntax:
jobs [options] jobID
To check the status jobs in the current shellsimply enter **jobs** in the CLI interface.
Here are some options you can use:

- **-l** lists process identifiers and information about them.
- **-n** lists jobs whose status has changed since the last notification.
- **-p** lists process identifiers only.

24. Order kill

Use the **kill command** to manually terminate an unresponsive program. It signals applications that are behaving badly and asks them to close their processes.

To kill a program, you need to know its process identification number (PID). If you don't know the PID, run the following command:

ps ux

Once you have determined the signal to be used and the program PID, enter the following syntax:

kill [signal_option] pid

There are **64 signals** you can use, but these two are among the most common:

SIGTERM tells a program to stop running and gives it time to save all its progress. The system will use it by default if you do not specify the signal when entering the kill command.

SIGKILL forces programmes to stop, and you will lose any unsaved progress.

For example, the program's PID is **63773** and you want to force it to stop:

kill SIGKILL 63773

25. Ping command

The **ping command** is one of the most commonly used basic Linux commands for checking a network or server can be reached. It is also used to solve various connectivity problems.

Here is the general format:

ping [option] [hostname or_IP_address]

For example, you want to know if you can connect to **Google** and measure its response time:

ping google.com

26. wget command

The Linux command line lets you download files from the Internet using the **wget command**. It runs in the background without interfering with other running processes.

The **wget** command retrieves files using the HTTP, HTTPS and FTP protocols. It can perform recursive downloads, which transfer parts of websites by following directory structures and links, creating local versions of web pages.

To use it, enter the following command:

wget [option] [url]

For example, enter the following command to download the latest version of WordPress:

wget https://wordpress.org/latest.zip

27. uname command

The uname or unix name command can used to obtain detailed information about your Linux system and hardware. This information includes the machine name, operating system and kernel. To run this command, simply enter **uname** in your CLI.

Here is the basic syntax:

uname [option]

These are the acceptable options to use:

- **a** displays all the information about the system.
- **s** prints the kernel name.
- **n** prints the host name of the system node.

28. Top order

The **top command** in the Linux terminal displays all running processes and a dynamic real-time view of the current system. It summarises the use of resources,

from the CPU to memory usage.
The **top** command can also help you identify and terminate a process that is using too many system resources.
To execute the command, simply enter **top** in the CLI.

29. Order history

With the **history** command, the system will list up to 500 previously executed commands, allowing you to re-use them without having to re-enter them. Remember that only users with **sudo** privileges can run this command. How this utility works also depends on the Linux shell you are using.
To run it, enter the command below:
history [option]
This command supports a number of options, such :
- **c** clears the entire history list.
- **d offset** deletes the entry from the history at the **OFFSET** position.
- added historical lines.

30. Manual control

The **man** command provides a user manual for all the commands or utilities you can run in the terminal, including name, description and options.
It comprises nine sections:
Executable programs or shell commands
System calls
Calls to the library
Games
Special reports
File formats and conventions
System administration commands
Core routines
Miscellaneous
To display the full manual, enter :
man [order_name]
For example, you want to access the manual for the **ls** command **:**
man ls
Enter this command if you wish to specify the section displayed :
man [option] [section_number] [order_name]
For example, you want to consult section 2 of the manual for the **ls** command **:**
man 2 ls

31. Command echo

The **echo** command is a built-in utility that displays a line of text or a string of characters on the standard output. Here is the basic syntax:
echo [option] [string]
For example, you can display the text **Hostinger Tutorials** by entering :
echo "Hostinger Tutorials
This command supports a number of options, such as :
- **n** displays the output without the new end line.
- his allows us to interpret the following backslashes:

\a plays an audible alert.

\b removes spaces between text.
\lt doesn't produce anything else.

- **E** displays the default option and disables backslash interpretation.

32. Zip and unzip commands

Use the **zip** command to compress your files into a **ZIP** file, a universal format commonly used under Linux. It can automatically choose the best compression ratio.

The **zip** command is also useful for archiving files and directories and disk usage.

To use it, enter the following syntax:

zip [options] zipfile filel file2....

For example, you have a file named **note.txt** that you want to compress into **archive.zip** in the current directory :

zip archive.zip note.txt

The **unzip command**, on the other hand, extracts zipped files from an archive. Here is the general format:

unzip [option] filename.zip

For example, to decompress a file called **archive.zip** in the current directory, enter :

unzip archive.zip

33. Command hostname

Run the **hostname** command to find out the host name of the system. You can run it with or without options. Here is the general syntax:

hostname [option]

There are many optional flags to use, including :

- **a** or **-alias** displays the hostname alias.
- **A** or **-all-fqdns** displays the fully qualified domain name (FQDN) of the machine.
- **i** or **-ip-address** displays the machine's IP address.

For example, enter the following command to find out the IP address of your computer:

hostname -i

34. useradd, userdel commands

Linux is a multi-user system, which means that several people can use it simultaneously. The **useradd** command **is used** to create a new account, the **passwd** command is used add a password. Only people with root or **sudo** privileges can run the **useradd** command.

When you use the **useradd** command, it makes a few major changes:

Modifies the **/etc/passwd**, **/etc/shadow**, **/etc/group** and **/etc/gshadow** files for newly created accounts.

Creates and populates a personal directory for the user.

Defines the permissions and owners of files in the home directory.

Here is the basic syntax:

useradd [option] username

To set the password :

passwd password_combination

For example, to add a new person named John, enter the following command at

the same time:
useradd John
passwd 123456789
To delete user account, use the **userdel** command:
userdel username

35. apt-get command

apt-get is a command-line tool for managing APT (Advanced Package Tool) libraries under Linux. It lets you retrieve information and packages from authenticated sources to manage, update, remove and install software and its dependencies.
The **apt-get** command requires **sudo** or root privileges.
Here is the main syntax:
apt-get [options] (command)
Here are the most common commands you can add to **apt-get** :
update synchronises the package files from their sources.
upgrade installs the latest version of all installed packages.
check updates the package cache and checks for faulty dependencies.

36. nano, vi, jed commands

Linux allows users to edit and manage files using a text editor, such as **nano**, **vi** or **jed**. **nano** and **vi** are supplied with the operating system, while **jed** must be installed.
The **nano command** designates keywords and works with most languages. To use it, enter the following command:
nano [filename]
vi uses two operating modes: **insert** and **command**. **insert** is used to edit and create a text file. The **command**, on the other hand, is used perform operations such as saving, opening, copying and pasting a file.
To use **vi** on a file, enter :
vi [filename]
jed has a drop-down menu interface that allows users to perform actions without having to enter combinations or commands on the keyboard. Like **vi**, it has modes for loading modules or plugins to write specific texts.
To open the program simply enter **jed** on the command line.

37. Alias and unalias commands

The alias command is used to create a shortcut with the same functionality as a command, file name or text. When executed, it tells the command interpreter to replace one string with another.
To use the **alias** command, enter the following syntax:
alias Name=Chame
For example, you want to make **k** the alias for the **kill** command:
alias k='kill'
The **unalias** command, on the other hand, deletes an existing alias.
Here's what the general syntax looks like:
unalias [alias_name]

38. Order on

The switch user or **su** command allows you to run a program as different user. It modifies the administrative compie in the current connection session. This command is particularly useful for accessing the system via **SSH** or for using the GUI display manager when the root user is not available.

Here is the general syntax of the command:

su [options] [username [argument]]

When run without options or arguments, the **su** command is executed with root privileges. It will ask you to authenticate and temporarily use **sudo** privileges.

Here are some acceptable options to use:

- **p** or **-preserve-environment** keeps the same shell environment, consisting HOME, SHELL, USER and LOGNAME.
- **s** or **-shell** allows you to specify a different shell environment to run.
- **l** or **-login** executes a connection script to change to another user name. To run it, you need to enter the user's password.

39. htop control

The **htop** command is an interactive program that monitors system resources and server processes in real time. It is available on most Linux distributions, and you can install it using the default package manager.

Compared with **the top** command, **htop** offers many improvements and additional functions, such as the use of the mouse and visual indicators.

To use it, run the following command:

htop [options]

You can also add options such as :

- **d** or **-delay** indicates the delay between updates in tenths of seconds.
- **C** or **-no-color** activates monochrome mode.
- **h** or **-help** displays the help message and quits.

40. Order ps

The process status or **ps** command provides an overview of all the processes running on your system. The static results come from the virtual files in the **/proc** file system.

Executing the **ps** command without any options or arguments gives you the list of processes currently running in the shell, and the list of processes currently running in the shell:

The unique process identifier (**PID**)

Terminal type (**TTY**)

Operating time (**TIME**)

The command that starts the process (**CMD**)

Here are some acceptable options you can use:

- **T** displays all the processes associated with the current shell session.
- **username** lists the processes associated with a specific user.
- **A** or **-e** displays all current processes.

Tips and tricks

Here are some tips and tricks you can use to manage your Linux system:

Enter the **clear** command to clear terminal screen.

Press the **Tab** key to automatically fill in the form after entering a command with an argument.

Use **Ctrl + C** to end a command in progress.

Press **Ctrl + Z** to pause a command in progress.
Use **Ctrl + S** to temporarily freeze your terminal.
Press **Ctrl + Q** to cancel the terminal freeze.
Use **Ctrl + A** to move to the start of the line.
Press Ctrl + E to reach the end of the line.
When you execute several commands on the same line, use (;) to separate them. You can also use **&&** to allow the next command to be executed only if the previous one has been executed successfully.
Did you know that you could edit a text file with Linux commands using SSH? Instead of editing a file locally and downloading it via FTP, you can edit the file instantly on your computer using the vim or nano command.

Use this table to quickly find the control you are looking for and how it works

Ordering	**Explanation**
Sudo	Executes a command with administrative privileges (superuser)
Pwd	Displays the current working directory
Cd	Changes the current directory
Ls	Lists files and directories in the current directory
Cat	Concatenates and displays the contents of files
Cp	Copying files and directories
Mv	Moves or renames files and directories
Mkdir	Creates a new directory
Rmdir	Deletes an empty directory
Rm	Deletes files and directories
Touch	Creates an empty file or updates the timestamp of an existing file
Locate	Search for files and directories in a pre-built database
Find	Search for files and directories in a specified location
Grep	Search for a pattern in files or input streams
Df	Displays disk space usage for file systems
From	Estimate^ use disk space for files and directories
Head	Displays the first part of the files
Tail	Displays the last part of the files
Diff	Compares files line by line
Ordering	**Explanation**
Tar	Archive files and directories in a single file
Chmod	Modifies file and directory permissions
Chown	Changes the owner of files and directories
Jobs	Lists active tasks
Kill	Sends a signal to terminate processes
Ping	Sends network requests to a specific IP address or domain name
Wget	Download files from the web
Uname	Displays system information

Top	Displays system resource usage in real time
History	Displays order history
Man	Displays the control manual pages
Echo	Displays the given arguments or variables
Zip	Creates a compressed zip archive from files
Unzip	Extracting files from a zip archive
Hostname	Displays or sets the host name of the system
Useradd	Create a new user account
User	Delete a user account
apt-get	Manages package management tasks
Nano	A text editor for the command line
Vi	A text editor for the command line
Jed	A lightweight text editor for the command line
Ordering	**Explanation**
Alias	Creates a shortcut or alias for a command
Unalias	Deletes an alias for a command

Linux commands allow you to carry out basic and administrative tasks quickly and efficiently from the terminal. This gives you greater flexibility on your system and access to functions that are not always available via a graphical user interface.

It is essential to learn the basic Linux commands to interact with your machine, especially if you are using a virtual private server (**VPS**). In most cases, each utility consists of three parts: a **command name**, a **flag** or **option,** and a **parameter** or **argument**.

This section covers 40 common commands, such as **apt- get** to install a package, **nano** to manipulate a file, **htop** to monitor running processes and **ls** to display a directory.

What is the basic Linux command?

One of the most commonly used Linux commands is cat (short for concatenate). This command allows you to create, display and combine files, as well as redirect the output (the contents of the entire file).

How many Linux commands does it have?

There are over 100 commands common to Linux and other similar operating systems.

3.2. Process handling

The basic process management operations are :

- process creation, fork() ;
- process identification, getpid() and getppid() ;
- termination of a process, exit() ;
- waiting for a child process to terminate: wait() ;
- process replacement, execve() and derivatives.

1 Process

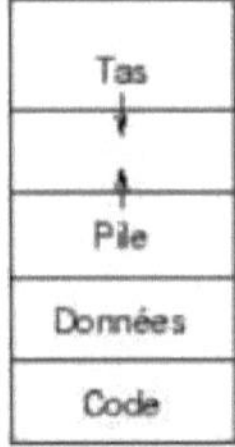

Figure 1: Organisation of the memory allocated to a process

A process is a running program.

Different resources are associated with a process.

In particular, a memory area is allocated to the process (see figure above). A process is unambiguously identified by an integer (pid, *process id*).

Unix is a multi-process system. Unix is a time-sharing system: *ready* processes are made to "run" concurrently; there is an impression of parallelism; this activity is called "process scheduling".

Processes are organised in a process tree. A particular process (init, with pid 1) is the root of this tree.

2 Process creation

System call

#include <sys/types.h>

#include <unistd.h>

pid_t fork (void) ;

Creates a new process (child process). This is an exact copy of the calling process.

fork () returns

- 0 in the child process ;
- the pid of the child in the parent process (-1 in the event of an error).

The use of fork() is illustrated in Figure 2

```
% cat creer_procesus.c
#include <stdio.h>
#include <sys/types.h>
#include <unistd.h>

int main (void) {
  pid_t pid ;

  pid = fork () ;

  if (pid == -1) {
    perror ("creation processus impossible") ;
    exit (1) ;
  }

  if (pid != 0)
    printf ("Je suis le père, j'ai créé le processus %d\n", pid) ;
  else
    printf ("Je suis le processus fils\n") ;
}

% ./creer_processus
Je suis le père, j'ai créé le processus 14602
```

```
Je suis le processus fils
```

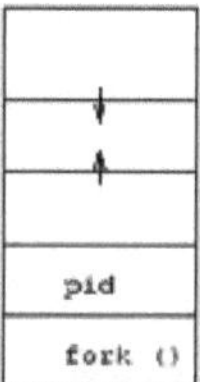

Figure 2: Use of the fork() primitive and state of process memory following the fork() call

3 Termination of the current process

The current process terminates automatically when it stops executing the main() function. The following primitives allow it to explicitly stop execution:

```
#include <unistd.h>

void _exit (int status) ;
void exit (int status) ;
```

These two primitives terminate the current process. The `status` parameter specifies a return code, between 0 and 255, to be sent to the parent process. By convention, in the event of normal termination, a process should return the value 0.

Before ending the execution of the process, `exit()` executes the "clean-up" functions of the standard libraries.

Exercise 1 *Explain the behaviour of the program shown in Figure 3.*

```
#include <stdio.h>
#include <sys/types.h>
#include <unistd.h>

int main (void)
{
  int i ;
  for (i=0 ; i < 4 ; i++) {
    int retour ;
    retour = fork () ;
    switch (retour) {
      case -1 : /* erreur */
        perror ("erreur fork\n") ;
        exit (1) ;
      case 0 : /* fils */
        printf ("fils : %d\n", i) ;
      default : /* pere */
        printf ("pere : \n") ;
    }
  }
}
```

Figure 3: What does this programme do?

Resolution.

This program uses the fork() function to child processes from a parent process. Here's how it works:

1. The `for` loop iterates four times, creating four processes.
2. At each iteration, the `fork()` function is called. This is what happens:

o If `fork()` succeeds, it creates a new child process identical to the parent process. The child process starts running from the point at which `fork()` was called.

o In the parent process, `fork()` returns the child process identifier (PID), which is a positive integer.

- In the child process, `fork()` returns 0.
- If `fork ( )` fails, no child process is created and -1 is returned to the parent process.

3. The code uses a `switch` instruction to manage the different cases:

- If `fork()` fails (return -1), an error is displayed.
- If `fork()` succeeds and the process is the child (return 0), it displays "child: i" where `i` is the value of the iteration.
- If `fork()` succeeds and the process is the parent (positive return), it displays "father: ".

4. The result will be a combination of output from the parent and child processes, which may appear in a different order depending on the operating system schedule.

In short, this program creates several processes (a parent and several children) and displays messages for each process created. The exact behaviour will depend on how the operating system schedules the processes.

Exercise 2 *Write a program that displays the integers from 0 to 3 using 4 different processes. This program must end after all 4 integers have been displayed.*

Resolution.

Here is an example of a C language program that creates four different processes to display integers from 0 to 3 :

```
#include <stdio.h>
#include <sys/types.h>
#include <unistd.h>
#include <stdlib.h>

int main() {
    for (int i = 0; i < 4; i++) {

        pid_t pid = fork();
        if (pid == -1) {
            perror("Erreur fork");
            exit(EXIT_FAILURE);
        } else if (pid == 0) {
            // Code exécuté par le processus fils
            printf("Processus fils %d : %d\n", i, i);
            exit(EXIT_SUCCESS); // Terminer le processus fils
        }
    }

    // Attendre que tous les processus fils se terminent
    for (int i = 0; i < 4; i++) {
        wait(NULL);
    }

    printf("Tous les processus ont terminé.\n");
    return 0;
}
```

In this programme :

- We use the `fork()` function to create four processes.
- Each child process displays its own integer (from 0 to 3).
- The parent process waits for all child processes to terminate using `wait(NULL)`.

Execution of this program will display the integers in ascending order and will end when all 4 integers have been displayed.

4 Process identity

A process is identified by its pid. It can know its father's pid.

The two primitives

```
#include <sys/types.h>
#include <unistd.h>

pid_t getpid(void);
pid_t getppid(void);
```

return the pid of the process and its parent respectively.

Example

```
% cat pid.c
#include <stdio.h>
#include <sys/types.h>
#include <unistd.h>

int
main (void)
{
  pid_t pid_fils ;

  switch (pid_fils = fork ()) {
    case -1 :
      perror ("Fork ") ;

      exit (1) ;
    case 0 : /* le fils */
      printf ("Je suis le fils, PID %d, PPID %d\n",
              getpid (), getppid ()) ;
      exit (0) ;
    default :  /* le  père */
      printf ("Je suis le pere, PID %d. Mon fils a le pid %d\n",
              getpid (), pid_fils);
      (void) wait (NULL) ;
      exit (0) ;
  }
}

% ./pid
Je suis le père, PID 8078. Mon fils a le pid 8079
Je suis le fils, PID 8079, PPID 8078
```

```
I am the father, PID 8078. My son has pid 8079
I am the son, PID 8079, PPID 8078
```

5 Waiting for a child process to terminate

The primitive

```
#include <sys/types.h>
#include <sys/wait.h>

pid_t wait (int *status) ;
```

suspends execution of the calling process until one of its children terminates. If a child process has already terminated, `wait()` returns the result immediately. wait() returns the pid of the child process if the return is due to the termination of a child process; -1 in the event of an error.

If status is not a null pointer, the status of the child process (value returned by exit()) is stored in the location pointed to by status.

More specifically:

- the low byte is a code indicating why the child process has stopped;
- if the child process has made a call to exit(), the preceding byte contains the return code.

This information can be accessed easily using the following macros defined in sys/wait.h. (Note that these macros use the status, not a pointer to it). :

WIFEXITED (status)

returns true if the status comes from a child process which has terminated normally;

WEXITSTATUS (status)

(if WIFEXITED (status) returns true) returns the return code of the child process passed to _exit() or exit() or the value returned by the main() function;

WIFSIGNALED (status)

returns true if the status comes from a child process which has terminated due to the reception of a ;

WTERMSIG (status)

(if WIFSIGNALED (status) returns true) returns the value of the signal which caused the child process to terminate.

Other macros are available; their documentation can be accessed at man 2 wait.

Example

```
% cat status_fils.c
#include <stdio.h>
#include <sys/wait.h>
#include <unistd.h>
#include <stdlib.h>

main (void)
{
  pid_t pid ;
  int status ;

  pid = fork () ;

  switch (pid) {
    case -1 :
      perror ("fork") ;
      exit (1) ;
    case 0 : /* le fils */
      printf ("processus fils\n") ;
      exit (2) ;
    default : /* le pere */
      printf ("pere: a cree processus %d\n", pid) ;
      wait (&status) ;
      if (WIFEXITED (status))
        printf ("fils termine normalement: status = %d\n",
                WEXITSTATUS (status)) ;
      else
        printf ("fils termine anormalement\n") ;
  }
}

% ./status_fils
pere: a cree processus 907
processus fils
fils termine normalement: status = 2
```

Exercise 3 *Write a program that displays, in order, the integers from 0 to 3 by 4 processes using the following structure;*

```
for (i=0 ; i < 4 ; i++) {
  switch (fork ()) {
    case -1 :
        ...
    case 0 :
        ...
    default :
        ...
  }
```

Resolution.

Here is an example of a C language program that creates four child processes and displays the integers from 0 to 3, each in a separate process:

```
#include <stdio.h>
#include <stdlib.h>
#include <unistd.h>
#include <sys/wait.h>

int main() {
    for (int i = 0; i < 4; ++i) {
        pid_t pid = fork();

        if (pid == -1) {
            perror("Erreur lors de la création du processus fils");
            exit(1);
        } else if (pid == 0) {
            // Code exécuté par le processus fils
            printf("Processus fils %d : Entier = %d\n", i + 1, i);
            exit(0);
        }
    }

    // Code exécuté par le processus parent
    for (int i = 0; i < 4; ++i) {
        wait(NULL);
    }

    printf("Tous les processus fils ont terminé.\n");

    return 0;
}
```

In this programme :

- We use a `for` loop to create four child processes.
- Each child process displays its number and the corresponding integer! (from 0 to 3).

- The parent process waits for all child processes to finish using the `wait()` function.

Don't forget to adapt this code to your specific environment and needs. I hope it helps you to display integers from 0 to 3 by 4 processes.

Exercise 4 [Trifork] *Write the function*

```
trifourche (void(*)(void), void(*)(void), void(*)(void)) ;
```

The process executing trifork (fi, f2, f3) generates processes executing functions fi, f2, and f3 respectively, and waits for the end of the generated processes to complete the function.

This function is used, for example, in the following context:

```
void fa (void)
{
  sleep (4) ;
  printf ("Fonction fa executee par le processus %d\n", getpid ()) ;
}

void fb (void)
{
  sleep (2) ;
  printf ("Fonction fb executee par le processus %d\n", getpid ()) ;
}

void fc (void)
{
  sleep (3) ;
  printf ("Fonction fc executee par le processus %d\n", getpid ()) ;
}

int main (void)
{
  trifourche (fa, fb, fc) ;
  printf ("Terminaison de main ()\n") ;
}
```

Resolution.

Here is an implementation of the trifork function in C that creates three child processes, executes the functions f1, f2 and f3 respectively, then waits for the end of these processes before terminating the function :

```
#include <stdio.h>
#include <stdlib.h>
#include <unistd.h>
#include <sys/wait.h>

// Signature de la fonction trifourche
void trifourche(void (*f1)(void), void (*f2)(void), void (*f3)(void)) {
    pid_t pid1, pid2, pid3;

    // Crée le premier processus fils
    pid1 = fork();
    if (pid1 == 0) {
        f1(); // Exécute la fonction f1
        exit(0);
    }

    // Crée le deuxième processus fils
    pid2 = fork();
    if (pid2 == 0) {
        f2(); // Exécute la fonction f2
        exit(0);
    }

    // Crée le troisième processus fils
    pid3 = fork();
    if (pid3 == 0) {
        f3(); // Exécute la fonction f3
        exit(0);
    }

    // Attends la fin des processus fils
     waitpid(pid1, NULL, 0);
     waitpid(pid2, NULL, 0);
     waitpid(pid3, NULL, 0);
}

// Exemple d'utilisation
void fa(void) {
    sleep(4);
    printf("Fonction fa exécutée par le processus %d\n", getpid());
}

void fb(void) {
    sleep(2);
    printf("Fonction fb exécutée par le processus %d\n", getpid());
}

void fc(void) {
    sleep(3);
    printf("Fonction fc exécutée par le processus %d\n", getpid());
}

int main(void) {
    trifourche(fa, fb, fc);
    printf("Terminaison de main()\n");
    return 0;
}
```

In this example :

- The `trifork` function creates three child processes, executes the `fi`, `f2` and `f3` functions and then waits for them to terminate.
- The `fa`, `fb` and `fc` functions are executed by the child processes with simulated sleep
.

Don't forget to adapt this code to your specific environment and needs. I hope it helps you understand and use the trifork function.

Exercise 5 [Multifork] *The multifork() function generalises the previous trifork() function.*

```
typedef int (*intint ) (int) ;

void multifourche (int n, intint f[]) ;
```

The `intint` *type is defined as "a pointer to a function returning integer to integer". The arguments to* `multifork()` *are an array of such functions and the size* `n` *of this array. Each of the functions is executed by a different process, which also displays the value returned by the function.*

Resolution.

The multifork() function generalises the trifork() function by accepting an array of functions pointing to functions returning integers. Here's how it works:

1. **Definition of `multifork()`**:

o The `multifork()` function takes two arguments: an integer `n` (the size of the array of functions) and an array of function pointers `f[]`.

o Each element of the array `f[]` is a function that returns an integer.

o The `multifork()` function executes each function in the `f[]` array in a separate process.

o After executing each function, the value returned by this function is displayed.

2. **Example of use**: Suppose we have three functions: `fi()`, `f2()`, and `f3()`, each returning an integer. Here's how we could use `multifork()`

```
#include <stdio.h>

  // Définition des fonctions f1(), f2(), et f3()
  int f1() { return 10; }
  int f2() { return 20; }
  int f3() { return 30; }

  // Définition de multifourche()
  void multifourche(int n, int (*f[])()) {
      for (int i = 0; i < n; i++) {
          int result = fi; // Appelle la fonction fi
          printf("Résultat de la fonction %d : %d\n", i + 1, result);
      }

  }

  int main() {
      int (*functions[3])() = {f1, f2, f3}; // Tableau de pointeurs de
  fonctions
      multifourche(3, functions); // Exécute les fonctions en parallèle
      return 0;
  }
```

In this example, multifork() executes f1(), f2(), and f3() in parallel, displaying the values returned by each. The result could be :

```
Résultat de la fonction 1 : 10
Résultat de la fonction 2 : 20
Résultat de la fonction 3 : 30
```

Note that the order in which the functions are executed may vary depending on the operating system and process planning.

Exercise 6 *Let sigma be a command with two arguments. sigma inf sup displays the sum of the integers from inf to sup.*

Noting that Z=a,b-a/2 i and Z>-a/2+i, b i can be calculated independently to compute sigma a b, develop a version of the sigma command using processes.

Resolution.

The "sigma" command seems to be a function that calculates the sum of the integers between two bounds, using processes. Here is an approach to developing such a version of the command:

1. Divide the interval [a, b] into two equal parts: [a, (a+b)/2] and [(a+b)/2 + 1, b].
2. Create two separate processes to calculate the sum of the integers in these two sub-intervals.
3. Wait for the two processes to finish and add up the results.

Here is an example of code in C to illustrate this approach:

```
#include <stdio.h>
#include <stdlib.h>
#include <unistd.h>
#include <sys/wait.h>

// Calcule la somme des entiers de 'start' à 'end'
int compute_sum(int start, int end) {
    int sum = 0;
    for (int i = start; i <= end; ++i) {
        sum += i;
    }
    return sum;
}

int main() {
    int a = 1; // borne inférieure
    int b = 10; // borne supérieure

    pid_t pid = fork();

    if (pid == -1) {
        perror("Erreur lors de la création du processus fils");
        exit(1);
    } else if (pid == 0) {
        // Code exécuté par le processus fils
        int mid = (a + b) / 2;
        int sum1 = compute_sum(a, mid);
        printf("Processus fils 1 : Somme de %d à %d = %d\n", a, mid, sum1);
        exit(sum1);
    } else {
        // Code exécuté par le processus parent
        int mid = (a + b) / 2;
        int sum2 = compute_sum(mid + 1, b);
        printf("Processus parent : Somme de %d à %d = %d\n", mid + 1, b,
sum2);

        int status;
        wait(&status);

        if (WIFEXITED(status)) {
            int result = WEXITSTATUS(status);
            printf("Somme totale : %d\n", sum2 + result);
        } else {
            printf("Le processus fils a terminé anormalement.\n");
        }
    }

    return 0;
```

Don't forget to adapt this code to your specific environment and needs. I hope this will help you develop your version of the "sigma" command with processes.

Exercise 7 *The following program is compiled into an executable named share :*

```
#include <stdio.h>
#include <unistd.h>
#include <fcntl.h>

int main (void)
{
  char buf [6] ;
  int fd ;

  fd = open ("foo", O_RDWR, 420) ;

  switch (fork ()) {
    case -1 :
      perror ("fork") ;
      exit (1) ;
    case 0 :
      printf ("%d caracteres ecrits\n", write (fd, "12345", 5)) ;
      break ;
    default :
      printf ("%d caracteres lus\n", read (fd, buf, 5)) ;
      buf [5] = '\0' ;
      printf ("Ligne lue : %s\n", buf) ;
      close (fd) ;
  }
}
```

Give the result of the following sequence of Unix commands:

```
% echo ABCDEFGH > foo
% ./partage
% cat foo
```

Resolution

The program provided here uses the fork() function to create a child process. Here's what happens when you execute the sequence of Unix commands you've given:

1. The `echo ABCDEFGH > foo` command writes the string "ABCDEFGH" to the "foo" file.
2. When you run `./share`, the C program is launched. Here's what happens: o The parent process (the one that ran `./share`) creates a child process `using fork()`.

o The child process executes the `write(fd, "12345", 5)` command, which writes the string "12345" to the "foo" file.

o The parent process executes the `read(fd, buf, 5)` command, which reads 5 characters from the "foo" file into the `buf` buffer.

o Finally, the parent process displays the line read using `printf("Line read: %s\n", buf)` .

3. When the program is run, the contents of the "foo" file will be "12345GH" (the 5 characters written by the child process, followed by the last 2 characters of the initial "ABCDEFGH" file).

7 Process code change

The primitive

```
#include <unistd.h>
int execve (char *filename, char *argv[], char *envp[]) ;
```

transforms the calling process into a new process. Note that this does not create a new process, but overlaps the old process with the new one.

The new process is built from an ordinary executable file whose name is pointed to by `filename`.

The `argv` parameter points to an array of character string pointers terminated by a `NULL` pointer. These strings constitute the list of arguments for the new process. By convention, `argv[0]` is always present and must be the name of the program to be executed.

The `envp` parameter is also a pointer to an array of string pointers terminated by a `NULL` pointer. These identify the environment variables that will be accessible from the new process. These strings are constructed using the :

||<|variable name||>| = ||<|variable value||>|

Descriptors open in the calling process remain open in the new process.

When the executed program starts, it is called as follows: (the `main ()` parameters `argc`, `argv` and `envp` are optional)

```
main (int argc, char *argv[], char *envp[])
```

`execve()` returns to the calling process only in the event of an error and then returns -1.

Example

```
% cat execl.c
#include <stdio.h>
#include <sys/types.h>
#include <sys/wait.h>
#include <unistd.h>
#include <stdlib.h>

char *path = "./exec2" ;
char *argval[] = {"exec2", "foo", "bar", NULL} ;

int main (int argc, char *argv[], char *envp[])
{
 pid_t pid ;
```

```
  switch (retour = fork()) {
    case -1 :
      perror ("fork") ;
      exit (1) ;
    case 0 :
      printf ("processus fils va exécuter exec\n") ;
      execve (path, argval, envp) ;
      perror ("execve") ;
      exit (1) ;
    default :
      printf ("père: a créé processus %d\n", retour) ;
      wait(0) ;
      printf ("père: a reçu terminaison fils\n") ;
  }
}

% cat exec2.c
#include <stdio.h>

int main (int argc, char *argv[])
{
 int i ;

 printf ("execution de exec2\n") ;
 printf ("exec2: %d arguments\n", argc) ;
 for (i=0 ; i<argc ; i++)
   printf ("exec2 argument %d: %s\n", i, argv[i]) ;

 exit (0) ;
}

% ./exec1
processus fils va exécuter exec
père: a créé processus 14625
exécution de exec2
exec2: 3 arguments
exec2 argument 0: exec2
exec2 argument 0: foo
exec2 argument 0: bar
père: a reçu terminaison fils
```

Other primitives are available; they are written using `execve()`. These are `execl()`, `execlp()`, `execle()`, `execv()`, and `execvp()`, whose prototypes are as follows:

```
#include <unistd.h>

int execl (const char *filename, const char *arg, ...) ;
int execlp (const char *cmdname, const char *arg, ...) ;
int execle (const char *filename char *arg , ..., char* const envp[]) ;
int execv (const char *filename, char *const argv[]) ;
int execvp (const char *cmdname, char *const argv[]) ;
```

They allow you to specify the arguments of the new process in form of a list of arguments (`arg` parameters) rather than an array of character strings (`argv` parameters), and/or to search for the program to be executed among the search paths (`$PATH` environment variable, `cmdname` parameters) rather than completely specifying its path (`filename` parameters), and so on.

8 Example of operation

We illustrate the use of the previous primitives on the execution of a command (command) by a Unix shell (sh).

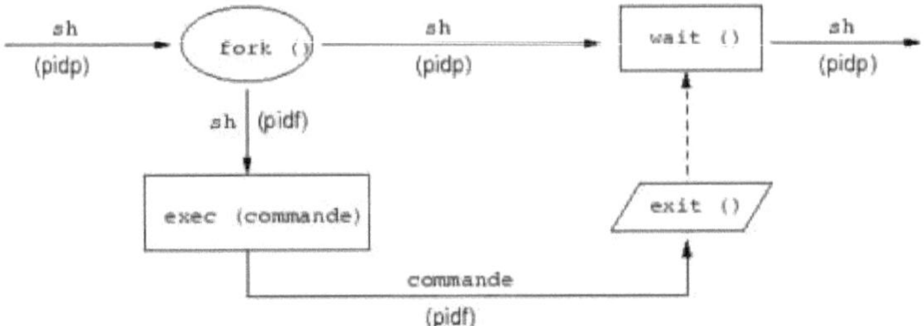

Figure 4: Executing a command in a Unix shell

Exercise 8

Question 1 Given the results of the following commands, draw the abbreviation of the processes of a command of the form `com1; com2; ...; comn`.

```
% who ; ps -f www ; date ; cd ; ls -F
phm       tty1      Apr 28 22:26
lambert   tty2      Apr 24 13:34
UID          PID  PPID  C STIME TTY       STAT   TIME CMD
phm          580   566  0 Apr28 pts/1     S      0:00 -csh
phm         1016   580  0 11:24 pts/1     R      0:00 ps -f www
Sat Apr 29 11:24:45 CEST 2000
INBOX                           ens/
auto/                           public_html/
bin/                            tex/
back/                           tmp/
dm/                             usr/
```

Resolution.

Here is the process tree for the given command:

```
who ; ps -f www ; date ; cd ; ls -F
```

1. The parent process executes the who command.
2. It then runs the ps -f www command.
3. It then executes the date command.
4. Then it tries execute the cd command, but as mentioned, cd is an internal shell command and cannot be executed directly via exec.
5. Finally, it executes the ls -F command.

The process tree looks like this:

```
who
 |
 +-- ps -f www

|    |
|    +-- date
|    |
|    +-- cd (non exécuté)
|    |
|    +-- ls -F
|
+-- date
|
+-- cd (non exécuté)
|
+-- ls -F
```

Note that the commands date, cd and ls -F are not executed due to the limitation mentioned. I hope this helps.

Question 2 Write a C program corresponding to the shell command

`who ; ps -f www ; date ; cd ; ls -F`

We will execute a series of `exec()`. As the `cd` command is an internal shell command, it cannot be launched directly by `exec()`.

Resolution.

To execute a series of shell commands in C, we can use the exec family of functions. Here is an example of a C program that executes the commands who, ps -f www, date, cd, and ls -f using execv :

```
#include <stdio.h>
#include <stdlib.h>
#include <unistd.h>
#include <sys/types.h>
#include <sys/wait.h>

int main() {
    pid_t child_pid;
    int status;

    // Crée un processus fils
    child_pid = fork();

    if (child_pid == 0) {
        // Code exécuté par le processus fils
        // Exécute la commande "who"
        char* who_args[] = {"who", NULL};
        execv("/usr/bin/who", who_args);
        perror("Erreur lors de l'exécution de who");
        exit(EXIT_FAILURE);
    } else if (child_pid > 0) {
        // Code exécuté par le processus parent
        // Attend la fin du processus fils
        wait(&status);

        // Exécute la commande "ps -f www"
        char* ps_args[] = {"ps", "-f", "www", NULL};
        execv("/bin/ps", ps_args);
        perror("Erreur lors de l'exécution de ps");
        exit(EXIT_FAILURE);
    } else {

        perror("Erreur lors de la création du processus fils");
        exit(EXIT_FAILURE);
    }

    // Les autres commandes (date, cd, ls -f) peuvent être ajoutées de
manière similaire
    // N'oubliez pas de gérer les erreurs pour chaque exécution de
commande.
    return 0;
}
```

Note that the cd command cannot be executed directly via exec, as it changes the working directory of the parent process. You will need to manage the directory change separately in your program. Good programming.

Question 3 Study the result of the following command (compare with the previous command)

```
% who & ps -f www & date & cd & ls -F &
phm      tty1     Apr 28 22:26
lambert  tty2     Apr 24 13:34
UID        PID  PPID  C STIME TTY      STAT   TIME CMD
phm        580   566  0 Apr28 pts/1    S      0:00 -csh
phm       1213   580  0 11:27 pts/1    R      0:00 ps -f www
phm       1214   580  0 11:27 pts/1    S      0:00 date
phm       1216   580  0 11:28 pts/1    S      0:00 ls -F
Sat Apr 29 11:27:35 CEST 2000
ChangeLog                       processus1.log
Makefile                        processus1.make
Readme                          processus1.tex
processus1.aux                  source
processus1.dvi                  tubes.tex
```

and write a C program corresponding to the shell commands

```
% who & ps -f www & date & cd & ls -F
```

et

```
% who & ps -f www & date & cd & ls -F &
```

and

Resolution.

First let's compare the two shell commands :

1. The first command is :

```
% who & ps -f www & date & cd & ls -F &
```

Here is the result:

```
% who & ps -f www & date & cd & ls -F &
```

Voici le résultat :

```
phm      tty1     Apr 28 22:26
lambert  tty2     Apr 24 13:34
UID        PID  PPID  C STIME TTY      STAT   TIME CMD
phm        580   566  0 Apr28 pts/1    S      0:00 -csh
phm       1213   580  0 11:27 pts/1    R      0:00 ps -f www
phm       1214   580  0 11:27 pts/1    S      0:00 date
phm       1216   580  0 11:28 pts/1    S      0:00 ls -F
Sat Apr 29 11:27:35 CEST 2000
ChangeLog                       processus1.log
```

This command runs several processes in parallel, displaying connected users, process information, the date and time, and the contents of the current directory.

2. The second command is :

```
% who & ps -f www & date & cd & ls -F
```

This command is similar to the first, but does not contain the last &. This means that the process will not run in the background. Instead, each command will wait for the previous one to finish before continuing. If we run it, we'll get similar results, but without the last process running in the background.

Now, here is a C program corresponding to the two shell commands (assuming we want to execute these commands in sequence) :

```
#include <stdio.h>
#include <stdlib.h>
#include <unistd.h>

int main() {
    // Exécute la commande "who"
    system("who");

    // Exécute la commande "ps -f www"
    system("ps -f www");

    // Exécute la commande "date"
    system("date");

    // Exécute la commande "cd" (ne fait rien dans ce contexte)
    chdir("/"); // Change le répertoire courant au répertoire racine

    // Exécute la commande "ls -F"
    system("ls -F");

    return 0;
}
```

This program executes the commands in the order specified, without running them in the background. Feel free to adapt it to your needs.

Exercise 9 *Give the implementation in the form of a C program of the following shell commands:*

```
tar xf foo.tar gee.txt && lpr gee.txt
```

et

```
tar xf foo.tar gee.txt || mail -s "il y a des erreurs" marquet@lifl.fr
```

Resolution.

Here is the C implementation for the two given shell commands:

1. **`tar xf foo.tar gee.txt && Ipr gee.txt`** :

○ This command extracts the gee.txt file from the foo.tar archive and sends it to the printer (lpr).

○ Here is the C implementation for this command:

```
#include <stdio.h>
#include <stdlib.h>
#include <unistd.h>

int main() {
    // Extrait le fichier gee.txt de l'archive foo.tar
    system("tar xf foo.tar gee.txt");

    // Envoie gee.txt à l'imprimante
    system("lpr gee.txt");

    return 0;
}
```

2. **`tar xf foo.tar gee.txt || mail -s "there are errors"marquet@lifl.fr`** :

○ This command extracts the gee.txt file from the foo.tar archive. If extraction fails (for example, if gee.txt does not exist in the archive), it sends an e-mail with the subject "there are errors" to the address .marquet@lifl.fr

○ Here is the C implementation for this command:

```
#include <stdio.h>
#include <stdlib.h>
#include <unistd.h>

int main() {
    // Extrait le fichier gee.txt de l'archive foo.tar
    int extraction_ok = system("tar xf foo.tar gee.txt");

    if (extraction_ok == 0) {
        // L'extraction a réussi
        printf("Extraction réussie !\n");
    } else {
        // L'extraction a échoué, envoie un e-mail
        system("mail -s \"il y a des erreurs\"
marquet@lifl.fr");
        printf("Envoi d'e-mail en cas d'erreur.\n");
    }

    return 0;
}
```

Don't hesitate to try out these programmes and adapt them to your needs.

Exercise 10 *Given the results of the following commands, draw the process tree for a command of the form* `com1 | com2 | ... | comn`.

```
% ps -f www | cat -n | tee foo | wc
      7      74     448
% cat foo
     1  UID        PID  PPID  C STIME TTY        STAT   TIME CMD
     2  phm        563   557  0 07:15 pts/1      S      0:00 -csh
     3  phm        672   563  0 08:29 pts/1      S      0:01 emacs
     4  phm       1169   563  0 11:26 pts/1      R      0:00 ps -f www
     5  phm       1170   563  0 11:26 pts/1      S      0:00 cat -n
     6  phm       1171   563  0 11:26 pts/1      S      0:00 tee foo
     7  phm       1172   563  0 11:26 pts/1      S      0:00 wc
```

Resolution.

To draw the process tree for this command, let's start by understanding the steps and connections between the different processes. Here's what each command does:

1. `% ps -f www`: Displays current processes in a detailed format.
2. `| cat -n`: Numbers each line of the previous output.
3. `| tee foo`: Redirects the output to a file named "foo".
4. `| wc`: Count the number of lines, words and bytes in the output.

Now let's look at the processes and their relationships:

- The initial process is `ps -f www`.
- The `cat -n` process is connected to the previous process via a pipe.
- The `tee foo` process is also connected to the initial process via another tube.
- Finally, the `wc` process is connected to the `tee foo` process.

Here is a simplified diagram of the process tree:

```
ps -f www
  |
cat -n
  |
tee foo
  |
  wc
```

Each arrow represents a connection between processes. Note that the initial process (ps -f www) is at the top of the tree, and the other processes branch off from there. I hope this helps you visualise the process tree.

Exercise 11 *The programme*

```
#include <stdlib.h>

int main (void)
{
  system ("ps") ;
}
```

has been compiled into an executable named `monps` *and placed in your home directory. The shell command*

```
% monps
```

is typed as soon as you log on. Which of the following statements are correct?

1. *Once the current processes have been displayed, the* `monps` *program terminates and the shell hands over to you.*
2. *Once the current processes have been displayed, the session ends and you are disconnected.*
3. *2 processes are displayed.*
4. *3 processes are displayed.*
5. *4 processes are displayed.*
6. *5 processes are displayed.*

Resolution.

The program you have compiled, monps, executes the shell command system("ps"), which displays the current processes. Now let's look at the statements and their answers:

1. **Once the current processes have been displayed, the monps program terminates and the shell hands over to you.**

   ○ **Answer:** True. Once the processes have been displayed, the monps program ends and you regain control of the shell.

2. **Once the current processes have been displayed, the session ends and you are disconnected.**

   ○ **Answer:** False. The session does not end automatically after the processes are displayed. You remain connected to the shell.

3. **2 processes are displayed.**

   ○ **Answer:** False. The number of processes displayed depends on the state of your system and the processes currently running. It may vary.

4. **3 processes are displayed.**

   ○ **Answer:** False. As mentioned above, the number of processes displayed can vary.

5. **4 processes are displayed.**

   ○ **Answer:** False. Once again, this depends on the context and the processes running on your system.

6. **5 processes are displayed.**

   ○ **Answer:** False. The exact number of processes displayed is not specified by the monps command.

In short, the first statement is true, while the others are false. Don't hesitate to consult a doctor if you have any questions about mental health, but you're in good hands when it comes to the system.

Exercise 12 *What are the differences between system* `()` *and* `execve()` *system calls?*

1. *There is no difference.*
2. `execve()` *lets run the same program several times.*
3. `execve()` *does not create a new process.*

Resolution.

The system() and execve() system calls are different in their operation and effects. Here are the distinctions between the two:

1. **system()** :

o The `system()` function is used to execute a shell command from a C program.

o It creates a new process to execute the specified command.

o Once the command has been executed, control reverts to the calling program.

o It uses the shell to interpret the command (for example, `/bin/sh`).

o It is easier to use, but less flexible.

2. **execve()** :

o The `execve()` function is used to execute a specific program from a C program.

o It replaces the image of the current process with that of the specified programme.

o It does not create a new process, but reuses the same process.

o After successful execution of `execve()`, the control does not return to the place where the function was called.

o It requires you to explicitly provide the full path to the program to be executed and the arguments.

In summary, system() is simpler for executing shell commands, while execve() is more powerful for executing specific programs by replacing the existing process.

Exercise 13 *To run an interactive* `shell` *process with pid p, issue the* `ps` *command.*

1. *Process p is transformed into a process running* `ps`.
2. *Process p creates a child f which executes* `ps` *and waits for p to terminate before terminating itself.*
3. *Process p creates a child f which executes* `ps`, *and p waits for this process f to terminate before resuming normal execution.*
4. *Process p creates a child f which executes* `ps`, *and resumes execution without waiting for f to terminate.*

Resolution.

Here is an example of a shell program that illustrates the scenario where the parent process creates a child that executes the ps command and waits for it to terminate before resuming normal execution:

```
#!/bin/bash

# Créer un processus fils

echo "Processus parent (PID $$) : Création du processus fils"
./fils.sh &

# Attendre que le processus fils se termine
wait

# Reprendre l'exécution normale du processus parent
echo "Processus parent : Exécution normale après la terminaison du
processus fils"
```

```
#!/bin/bash
#   Create a child process
```

```
echo "Parent process (PID $$) : Create child process" ./children.sh &
#  Wait for the child process to terminate wait
#  Resume normal execution of the parent process
echo "Parent process: Normal execution after termination of child
process".
```

The contents of the son.sh file (son process file) could be as follows:

```
#!/bin/bash

# Exécuter la commande ps
echo "Processus fils (PID $$) : Exécution de la commande ps"
ps
```

```
#!/bin/bash
#  Run the ps command
echo "Child process (PID $$): Execute ps command" ps
```

In this example, the parent process creates a child by launching the son.sh script. The parent waits for the child to finish before resuming normal execution. The child process simply executes the ps command.

Feel free to customise the content of the scripts to suit your specific needs.

Exercise 14 *You are already familiar with the `fork()` system call to create a process. There is another, `vfork()`, which behaves slightly differently: there is no copying of data and the stack, the new process shares them with its parent. The parent process is suspended until the child makes a call to `execve()` or terminates.*

What are the advantages and disadvantages of this system call? Give an example of a programme that would typically use `vfork()`.

Resolution.

The vfork() system call has specific advantages and disadvantages compared with the fork() system call. Here are the main differences:

1. **Advantages of vfork()** :

- **Less time and memory consuming**: Unlike fork(), vfork() does not copy the address space of the parent process. This means it is faster and requires less memory.
- **Use when executing a new program**: vfork() is designed to be used when the child process intends to call an overlay primitive (such as exec*). It shares the address with the parent process until it executes a new program image.
- **No copying of memory segments**: vfork() does not duplicate the code, data and stack segments of the parent process, which makes it more efficient.

2. **Disadvantages of vfork()** :

- **Unpredictable behaviour**: If the child process modifies the shared address space before calling exec*, this can lead to unexpected results.
- **Limited use**: vfork() is mainly useful for exec* calls. For other uses, it can be dangerous and unpredictable.

Here is an example of a C program using vfork() :

```
#include <stdio.h>
#include <stdlib.h>
#include <unistd.h>

int main() {
    pid_t child_pid = vfork();

    if (child_pid == 0) {
        // Code du processus fils
        printf("Processus fils : PID = %d\n", getpid());
        // Appel à exec* ou _exit ici
        _exit(0);
    } else if (child_pid > 0) {
        // Code du processus parent
        printf("Processus parent : PID = %d\n", getpid());
        // Attendre que le processus fils se termine
        wait(NULL);
    } else {
        perror("Erreur lors de vfork()");
        exit(EXIT_FAILURE);
    }

    return 0;
}
```

Don't forget that vfork() is rarely used directly, as modern copy-on-write (COW) techniques have reduced vfork()'s initial advantage.

3.3. Managing users and groups

Under Linux, group information is stored in the /etc/group file. You can use commands to create a group, add a user to a group, display the list of users in the group and remove a user from a group.

What is a Linux group?

A Linux or GNU/Linux user group, as well as GNU/Hurd, or even simply GNU, is a group of computer users - often a local association, sometimes a national one - within which users and supporters of the GNU/Linux operating system come together.

What is a user under Linux?

Any individual who needs to interact with a Linux system will need to identify themselves. The authenticated user will be recognised by a unique name and a unique ID.

(user ID). Information about users is stored in the /etc/passwd file.

How do I display the users in a group under Linux?

How do you list all the members of a group?

To list all the members of a group, use the **getent** command followed by the group name. The output shows the name of the group, its ID and the member users. If the output is empty, the group does not exist.

How do I assign a user to a Linux group?

To add a user to a group, use the **usermod** command with the **-aG** options. The options are explained below:

-G: new list of additional GROUPS.

-a: append mode for modifying user configuration.

How do I create a user on Linux?

Procedure

1. To **create a group**, use the **groupadd** command. ...
2. To add a member to an additional **group**, use the **usermod** command to list

the additional **groups** of which the **user** is currently a member and the additional **groups** of which the **user** is due to become a member.

3.4. Redirecting flows and creating shell scripts

Many Bash commands return a result. By default, the returned result will be displayed directly in the Terminal. Often, however, we want to ensure that the result of a command is stored in a file or reused for another command. We can do this by using input and output redirections.

First of all, you need to know that each order is associated with three flows:

1. The standard input (or stdin) which corresponds to input 0 ;
2. The standard output (or stdout) which corresponds to input 1 ;
3. The standard error output (stderr) which corresponds to input 2.

Standard output and redirection

Most commands that return a result will do so via input 1. By default, standard output directs the result to the current display (the Terminal). You can use a closing chevron> to ask standard output to direct the result to a file using the following syntax: command> my_file.txt. Here, the result of the "command" command will be directed to the file "my_file.txt".

```
Pierres-MacBook-Pro:~ pierre$ pwd
/Users/pierre
Pierres-MacBook-Pro:~ pierre$ ls > desktop/test.txt #Enregistre le résultat de ls dans un fichier "
test.txt" sur le bureau
```

In the example above, we redirect the result of an ls command (which displays the different items in a directory) to a file called "test.txt" on our desktop.

Please note one thing: when you use> , the result stored in the file will replace the previous contents of the file. To add the result after the content already in the file, we will use a double chevron .>>

```
Pierres-MacBook-Pro:~ pierre$ pwd
/Users/pierre
Pierres-MacBook-Pro:~ pierre$ ls >> desktop/test.txt
```

Please also note that if the redirection file mentioned does not exist, it will be automatically created.

Standard error output and redirection

The standard error output manages the display of errors that may be returned when a command cannot, for one reason or another, do its job (bad syntax on our part, etc.).

By default, standard output redirects error messages to the current display, which means that errors will be displayed directly in the Terminal for us.

Sometimes we want to hide errors from users because some errors may contain sensitive information or may not be relevant to the user. In these cases, we can redirect the standard output to a file using the syntax command 2> my_file or command 2>> my_file as before.

```
Pierres-MacBook-Pro:~ pierre$ pwd
/Users/pierre
Pierres-MacBook-Pro:~ pierre$ ls > desktop/test.txt 2>desktop/erreur.txt
```

Note that "2" represents the standard error output. The numbers are useful here to differentiate between the different entries. The integers 0, 1 and 2 are called file descriptors.

We can also redirect the standard error output to the standard output of the command using the command syntax 2>&1. This can be useful if you have previously defined a redirection for the standard output.

Standard entry and redirection

Most commands accept incoming data that will tell them what to do from what is known as standard input. By default, standard input retrieves data from the keyboard. Here again, we can redirect standard input so that it accepts data stored in files. To do this, this time we're going to use an opening chevron< like this: command < my_file.txt.

```
Pierres-MacBook-Pro:~ pierre$ pwd
/Users/pierre
Pierres-MacBook-Pro:~ pierre$ ls > desktop/test.txt 2>desktop/erreur.txt
Pierres-MacBook-Pro:~ pierre$ sort < desktop/test.txt
Applications
Creative Cloud Files
Desktop
Documents
Downloads
Library
Movies
Music
Pictures
Public
```

spell whose role is to sort data in alphabetical order by default and return the result.

Of course, there's nothing to stop us redirecting both standard input and standard output:

```
Pierres-MacBook-Pro:~ pierre$ pwd
/Users/pierre
Pierres-MacBook-Pro:~ pierre$ ls > desktop/test.txt 2>desktop/erreur.txt
Pierres-MacBook-Pro:~ pierre$ sort < desktop/test.txt > desktop/ls_trie.txt
```

Here, we pass our "test.txt" file to the sort command and redirect its result to another file called "ls_trie.txt".

Connecting several controls together

Redirecting the result of a command to a file rather than to the current display is not the only type of redirection we can do with Bash. We can also directly inject the result one command into another. This is a very useful and powerful feature. To do this, we simply use a vertical bar| between our different commands.

For example, we can pass the result of an ls -l command to an sort command in one line like this:

```
Pierres-MacBook-Pro:~ pierre$ sort | ls -l
total 0
drwxr-xr-x   3 pierre  staff    96 Jul 18 23:35 Applications
drwxrwxr-x@  3 pierre  staff    96 Jul 16 09:22 Creative Cloud Files
drwx------+ 43 pierre  staff  1376 Jul 28 15:33 Desktop
drwx------+  4 pierre  staff   128 Jun 12 11:09 Documents
drwx------+ 14 pierre  staff   448 Jul 23 20:09 Downloads
drwx------@ 67 pierre  staff  2144 Jul 18 23:27 Library
drwx------+  4 pierre  staff   128 Jun  9 19:07 Movies
drwx------+  4 pierre  staff   128 Jun 13 13:15 Music
drwx------+  5 pierre  staff   160 Jul 16 09:32 Pictures
drwxr-xr-x+  4 pierre  staff   128 Jun  6 13:48 Public
```

Note: command redirection as described above is similar in concept to the command substitution described above. However, the processes used are not the same and the language does not treat these two operations in the same way. The concepts used here are relatively specific and complex to understand, so we won't go into them any further in this book.

Summary table of redirections

Ordering	Definition
C > f	Executes the "C" command and redirects its standard output to file "f", overwriting its contents or creating it if it does not exist.
C >> f	Executes the C command and redirects its standard output to the end of file f
C 2> f	Executes the C command and redirects its standard error output to file f, overwriting its contents or creating f if it does not exist.
C 2>> f	Executes the C command and redirects its standard error output to the end of f.
C 2>&1	Executes the C command and redirects its standard error output to its standard output.
Ordering	**Definition**
C < f	Executes the C command, passing the contents of f to its standard input.
C1 | C2	Executes command C1 and injects its result (the contents of its standard output) into the standard input of command C2.

Linux/Shell: Redirection flows

With the Linux console, the operation is always the same:

you type the command (for example cat, ls, du) ;

the result is displayed in the console.

However, it is possible to redirect this result. Instead of the result being displayed in the console, you can send it elsewhere: to a file or as input to another command to perform "command strings, using special symbols called *redirection streams*, 1) > and >>: redirect the result to a file

The simplest manipulation we are about to see will allow you to **write the result** of a **command to a file**, instead of displaying it in the console.

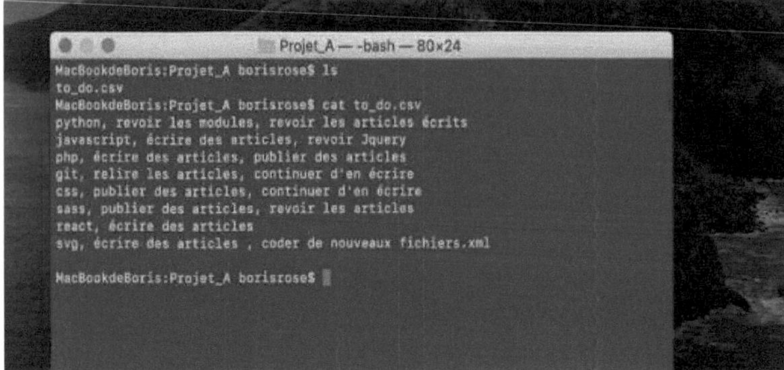

> : redirect to a new file

Suppose we want to write all the first fields to a file (e.g. python, git, css). This is where the**>** symbol (known as a **chevron**) comes into play. This symbol is used redirect the result of the command to the file of your choice.

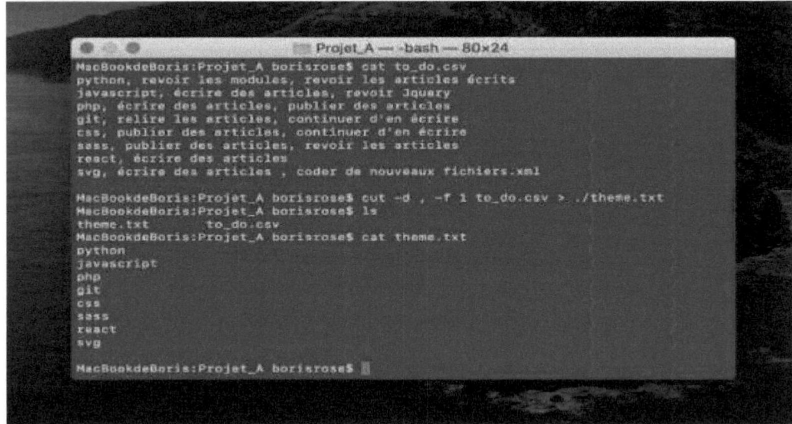

>> redirect to the end of a file

The double chevron>> is also used to redirect the result to a file, but this time to the end of the file. There is no risk of overwriting the file if it already exists. If the file does not exist, it will be created automatically.

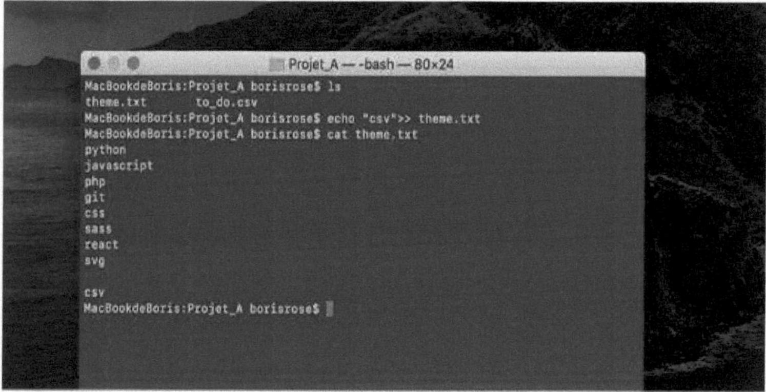

2) 2>, 2>> and 2>&1: redirect errors

All commands produce two different data streams: **standard output**: for all messages (except errors);

error output: for all errors.

Let's take a concrete example to see how it works.

Let's say you cat the to_do.csv file to display its contents. There are two possibilities:

if all goes well, the result (the contents of the file) is displayed on the standard output ;

if there is an error, it is displayed in the error output.

By default, everything is displayed in the console: standard output as well as error output. This explains why you couldn't tell the difference between these two outputs until now: they looked identical.

Redirect errors to a separate file

You might want to save the errors in a separate file so that you don't forget them and can analyse them later.

To do this, we use the 2> operator.

Let's make a second redirection at the end of this command:

```
Projet_A — -bash — 80×24
MacBookdeBoris:Projet_A borisrose$ ls
theme.txt       to_do.csv
MacBookdeBoris:Projet_A borisrose$ cut -d , -f >> to_do.txt 2>> erreur.txt
MacBookdeBoris:Projet_A borisrose$
```

```
Projet_A — -bash — 80×24
MacBookdeBoris:Projet_A borisrose$ ls
theme.txt       to_do.csv
MacBookdeBoris:Projet_A borisrose$ cut -d , -f >> to_do.txt 2>> erreur.txt
MacBookdeBoris:Projet_A borisrose$ ls
erreur.txt      theme.txt       to_do.csv       to_do.txt
MacBookdeBoris:Projet_A borisrose$ cat erreur.txt
cut: option requires an argument -- f
usage: cut -b list [-n] [file ...]
       cut -c list [file ...]
       cut -f list [-s] [-d delim] [file ...]
MacBookdeBoris:Projet_A borisrose$
```

Merging outputs

It is possible to merge the outputs into a single file. Use the following code: 2>&1. This has effect of redirecting all the error output into the standard output.

I told you that it was possible to use 2>> to redirect errors to the end of an error . However, it is not possible to write 2>>&1. In fact, the 2>&1 symbol will send errors to the same file and **in the same way** as standard output.

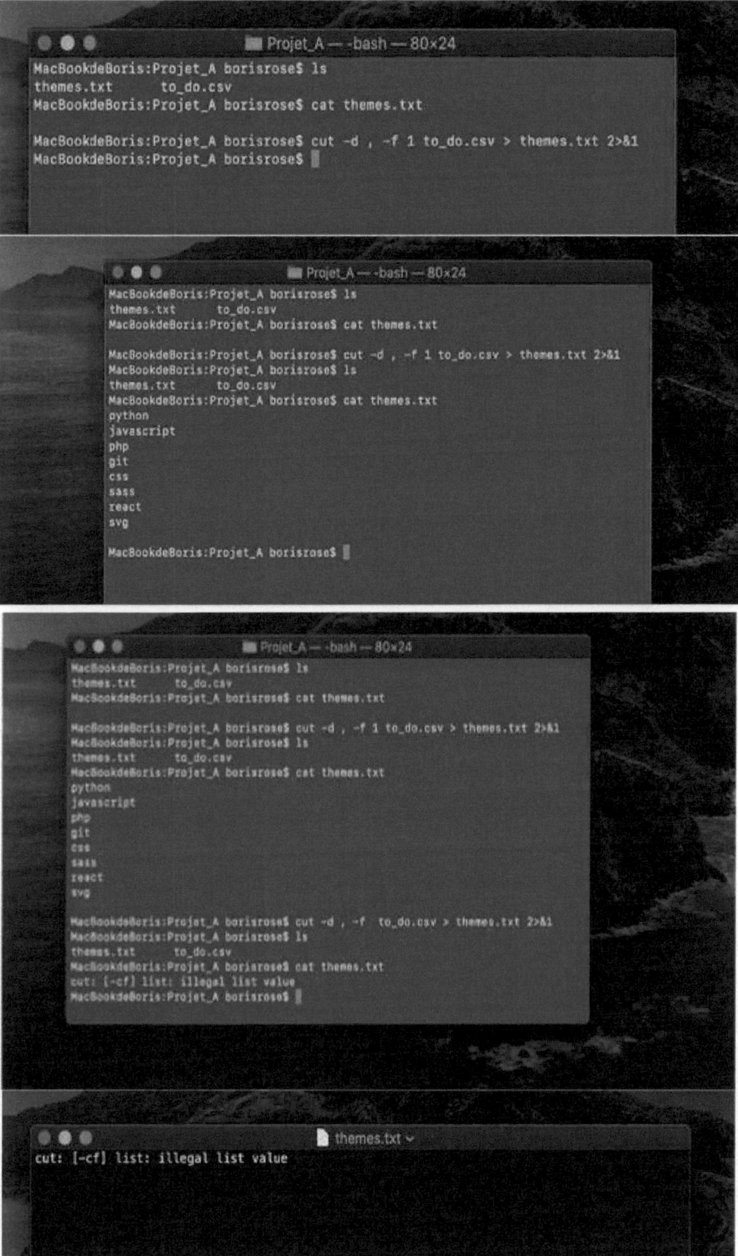

3) < and< <: read from a file or the keyboard

For the moment, we've only redirected the **output of** the commands. We've decided where to send messages from these commands. Now we are going to choose where the **input** to a command comes from. So far, the input has come from the command parameters, but we can now make it come from a file or keyboard input.

< read from a file

The opening chevron< (not to be confused with the closing chevron) is used indicate where the input sent to the command comes from.

Let's take an example: the cat command

```
MacBook-de-Boris:Projet_A borisrose$ cat < to_do.csv
python, revoir les modules, revoir les articles écrits
javascript, écrire des articles, revoir Jquery
php, écrire des articles, publier des articles
git, relire les articles, continuer d'en écrire
css, publier des articles, continuer d'en écrire
sass, publier des articles, revoir les articles
react, écrire des articles
svg, écrire des articles , coder de nouveaux fichiers.xml

MacBook-de-Boris:Projet_A borisrose$
```

This display the contents of the file sent as input.

Writing cat < to_do.csv is exactly the same as writing cat to_do.csv in appearance. The result is the same, but what happens behind it is very different.

If you write cat to_do.csv, the cat command will receive as input the name of the to_do.csv file, which it will then open to display its contents.

If you write cat < to_do.csv, the cat command receives **the contents** of to_do.csv which it simply displays in the console. The shell is responsible for sending the contents of to_do.csv to the cat command.

<< read from the keyboard progressively

The opening double chevron<< does something quite different: it you send content to a command using your keyboard. This can be very useful.

```
Projet_A — -bash — 80×24
Last login: Sun Feb 13 11:37:52 on ttys001

The default interactive shell is now zsh.
To update your account to use zsh, please run `chsh -s /bin/zsh`.
For more details, please visit https://support.apple.com/kb/HT208050.
MacBook-de-Boris:~ borisrose$ cd Desktop && cd Projets_Shell && cd Projet_A
MacBook-de-Boris:Projet_A borisrose$ ls
themes.txt      to_do.csv
MacBook-de-Boris:Projet_A borisrose$ sort -n << STOP
> 12
> 1
> 5
> 20
> STOP
1
5
12
20
MacBook-de-Boris:Projet_A borisrose$
```

So after the sort -n << STOP command, the console will prompt you to type text. As sort -n is used to sort numbers, we're going to write numbers, one per line (pressing the Enter key each time).

When you have finished, press STOP to stop typing.
All the text you have written is then sent to the command (sort in this case) which processes it as input. The sort command sorts the numbers.
In addition, the word STOP can be replaced by anything you like.
When you type the command, you can use any word you like. The important thing is that you define a keyword that will be used to indicate the end of the input. You are under no obligation to write this word in capitals.
You can combine these symbols with those seen above. For example :

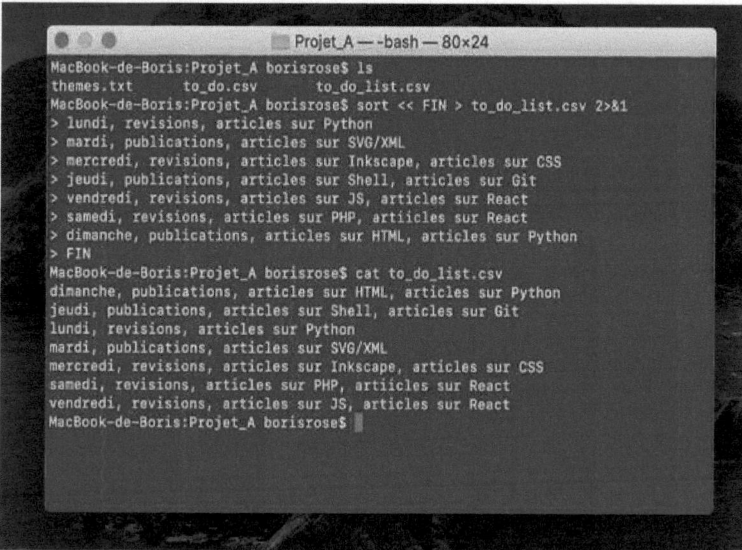

|: chain orders

Let's move on now to the most interesting symbol that you will use most often: the **pipe|** which can be used to chain commands.
The pipe| is not a symbol that we used to writing. On a French AZERTY keyboard, for example, you can write it by combining the Alt Gr + 6 keys, and on a Belgian keyboard, Alt Gr + 1. On a Mac keyboard, it's Alt + Shift + L.
"Chain commands together? This means connecting the output of one order to the input of another.
In other words, **everything that comes out of commandel is immediately sent to command2**. And you can chain commands like this indefinitely.
Example:

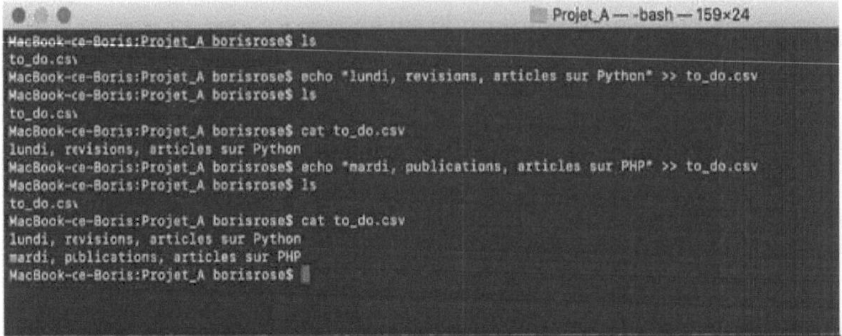

```
Projet_A — -bash — 159×24
MacBook-ce-Boris:Projet_A borisrose$ ls
to_do.csv
MacBook-ce-Boris:Projet_A borisrose$ echo "lundi, revisions, articles sur Python" >> to_do.csv
MacBook-ce-Boris:Projet_A borisrose$ ls
to_do.csv
MacBook-ce-Boris:Projet_A borisrose$ cat to_do.csv
lundi, revisions, articles sur Python
MacBook-ce-Boris:Projet_A borisrose$ echo "mardi, publications, articles sur PHP" >> to_do.csv
MacBook-ce-Boris:Projet_A borisrose$ ls
to_do.csv
MacBook-ce-Boris:Projet_A borisrose$ cat to_do.csv
lundi, revisions, articles sur Python
mardi, publications, articles sur PHP
MacBook-ce-Boris:Projet_A borisrose$
```

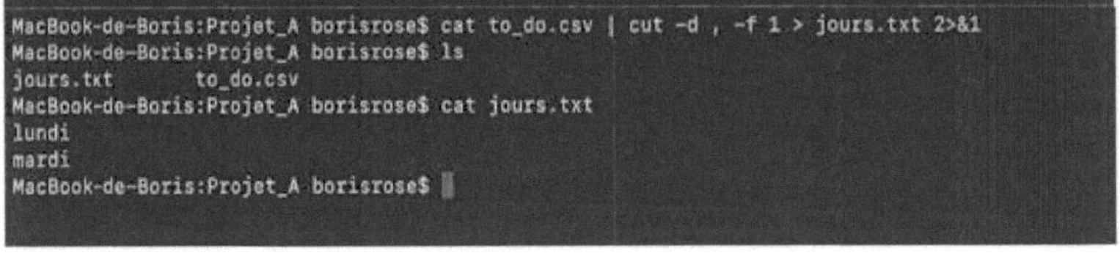

```
MacBook-de-Boris:Projet_A borisrose$ cat to_do.csv | cut -d , -f 1 > jours.txt 2>&1
MacBook-de-Boris:Projet_A borisrose$ ls
jours.txt       to_do.csv
MacBook-de-Boris:Projet_A borisrose$ cat jours.txt
lundi
mardi
MacBook-de-Boris:Projet_A borisrose$
```

Chapter 4

Unix/Linux system administration

4.1. Installing the Unix/Linux operating system[11]

Console mode installation (UNIX and Linux)

Run the installation in console mode if you want to supplement the installation options with a series of menus and prompts in a text-based user interface.

Before you start

Obtain the installation package for your operating system and extract the contents. Consult the access rule for deployment engine (DE). If a DE engine is already installed on the computer, save the engine.

Why and when to perform this task

Tip: During installation, you can enter quit in most of the menu screens to exit the installation programme. You can also enter back in some of the menu screens to return to the previous screen.

Procedure

To install Tivoli Netcool/OMNIbus in console mode :

1. Go to the directory where you extracted the contents of the installation module and run the following command: install.bin -i console

Tip: Use the -r command line option to save your installation settings in a response file called installer.properties which you can use later to run silent installations. The -r command line option must be the last option specified. If you are installing as the root user, no value is required for the -r option and the installer.properties file is generated in the directory containing the **install.bin** command. If you are installing as a non-root user, specify the full directory path and file name, for example: ./install.bin -r /tmp/installer.properties.

2. Enter a number corresponding to the language to be used for the installation procedure.
3. Read the Installation Information and press Enter when prompted. Press Enter to browse the licence agreement, then enter 1 to accept the agreement.
4. If you are installing as root, enter 1 to confirm that you want to install as root, then choose Install Deployment Engine. If a
5. deployment engine, the option to select the location of the deployment engine is not offered.

Option	Header
1	Accepts the default installation location for the DE engine.
2	Allows you to specify a different location. Use this option only for restricted systems where the root user cannot write to the /usr directory, for example Solaris sparse areas. The DE engine database files are installed in var/ibm/common/acsi and the remaining files are installed in the specified location. If the DE motor is already installed, the existing installation takes priority.

[11] McKusick, M. K., & Neville-Neil, G. V. (2004). *The Design and Implementation of the FreeBSD Operating System*. Addison-Wesley Professional.

6. If you are upgrading as a non-root user, you will not be prompted for a DE Engine location. The DE Engine is installed in */home/username/.acsi_hostname*, where *username* is the name of the user performing the upgrade. A symbolic link between /home/username/*.acsi_username*, which is the deployment engine installation directory in previous versions, points to */home/username/.acsi_hostname*.

7. If you are installing as root, the Autonomic Deployment Engine page is displayed. Choose the user access security rules you wish to apply to Deployment Engine :

Option	Description
1	Maintains current safety rules.
2	Limits use of the DE engine to the root user.
3	Limits use of the DE engine to the root user and a group of users. The group must already exist. You cannot create a user group at this stage.
4	Allows all users to use the DE engine. Users must be granted write access the DE database directory.

8. Specify and confirm an installation location for Tivoli Netcool/OMNIbus. This location becomes your NCHOME location. The default location is /opt/IBM/tivoli/netcool.

9. Enter 1 to install all functions or 2 to select a subset of functions to install. If you enter 2, enter a comma-separated list of numbers corresponding to the functions you do not need. Then review and confirm the feature selection.

10. Enter 2 to indicate that you do not wish to migrate data from an existing Tivoli Netcool/OMNIbus installation.

11. Check the summary of pre-installation tasks and that all mandatory functions have been selected. Then press Enter to start the installation. Once the process is complete, a confirmation message will appear.

12. Press Enter to exit the installation .

Results

Installation adds a number of files to your system.

What to do next

Check the messages in the installation log files. Before attempting to run Tivoli Netcool/OMNIbus, you must perform certain post-installation tasks. This includes installing and configuring required scanning and gateway components. If the installation fails, you may need to restart.

4.2. Configuring the system and network parameters

Network configurations under Linux

The aim is to become familiar with network configuration commands under Linux.

- Open a terminal and type the **ifconfig** command to find out and configure the network parameters. To find out the syntax of a command, there is an online manual for Linux. For example, to find out the syntax of **ifconfig**, type: **man ifconfig**.
- Determine the current configuration of your network interface (IP address, mask, MAC address).

```
user@ubuntu:~$ ifconfig
eth2      Link encap:Ethernet  HWaddr 00:0c:29:bd:32:a9
          inet adr:192.168.154.133  Bcast:192.168.154.255  Masque:255.255.255.0
```

- Use the **route -n** command to view your machine's routing table. Comment on the different lines and values. Explain exactly how your machine uses the routing table when it wants to send a packet to a machine on your LAN and to a remote machine.

```
user@ubuntu:~$ route -n
Table de routage IP du noyau
Destination     Passerelle      Genmask         Indic Metric Ref    Use Iface
192.168.154.0   0.0.0.0         255.255.255.0   U     0      0        0 eth2
0.0.0.0         192.168.154.2   0.0.0.0         UG    0      0        0 eth2
```

In the example above, the first line indicates that the PC is directly connected via its Ethernet 2 interface to the network address 192.168.154.0 (the PC's IP address is 192.168.154.133 and its mask is 255.255.255.0, so it is part of the 192.168.154.0 network). The second line indicates that to reach all the other addresses (0.0.0.0) you need to use the 192.168.154.2 gateway, exiting via Ethernet interface 2.

- Open a terminal and go to the **netkit** sub-directory of your working directory (**cd netkit**). Create a new sub-directory **tp** in **netkit** (**mkdir tp**). Go to this sub-directory (**cd tp**).
- To start a virtual machine, type the following command: **vstart pc1 --eth0=A**

This command starts the virtual machine named pc1 with a single Ethernet interface connected to a network named "A". A new window corresponding to this machine should appear.

- Start a second pc2 machine connected to the same Ethernet network in the same way.

vstart pc2 --eth0=A

- Use **the ifconfig** and **route** commands to configure the two PCs so that they can communicate and pc1 can act as a gateway for pc2 (check communication using the **ping** command).

```
pc1
pc1:~# ifconfig eth0 192.168.1.1 netmask 255.255.255.0 up
pc1:~# ping 192.168.1.2
PING 192.168.1.2 (192.168.1.2) 56(84) bytes of data.
64 bytes from 192.168.1.2: icmp_seq=1 ttl=64 time=13.7 ms
64 bytes from 192.168.1.2: icmp_seq=2 ttl=64 time=0.798 ms
64 bytes from 192.168.1.2: icmp_seq=3 ttl=64 time=0.556 ms
64 bytes from 192.168.1.2: icmp_seq=4 ttl=64 time=1.14 ms

--- 192.168.1.2 ping statistics ---
4 packets transmitted, 4 received, 0% packet loss, time 3006ms
rtt min/avg/max/mdev = 0.556/4.074/13.797/5.617 ms
pc1:~#
```

```
pc2:~# ifconfig eth0 192.168.1.2 netmask 255.255.255.0 up
pc2:~# route add default gw 192.168.1.1
pc2:~# route -n
Kernel IP routing table
Destination     Gateway         Genmask         Flags Metric Ref    Use Iface
192.168.1.0     0.0.0.0         255.255.255.0   U     0      0        0 eth0
0.0.0.0         192.168.1.1     0.0.0.0         UG    0      0        0 eth0
pc2:~# ping 192.168.1.1
PING 192.168.1.1 (192.168.1.1) 56(84) bytes of data.
64 bytes from 192.168.1.1: icmp_seq=1 ttl=64 time=13.3 ms
64 bytes from 192.168.1.1: icmp_seq=2 ttl=64 time=0.571 ms
64 bytes from 192.168.1.1: icmp_seq=3 ttl=64 time=0.542 ms
64 bytes from 192.168.1.1: icmp_seq=4 ttl=64 time=0.559 ms

--- 192.168.1.1 ping statistics ---
4 packets transmitted, 4 received, 0% packet loss, time 2998ms
rtt min/avg/max/mdev = 0.542/3.757/13.358/5.543 ms
pc2:~#
```

- To stop the virtual machines, type the command **vhalt pc1** (or pc2). You can also delete the files created by NetKit in the **tp** sub-directory.

A fuller explanation of how NetKit works and how to use its commands can be found at: http://wiki.netkit.org/index.php/Labs Official#Introduction

4.3 Managing services and software packages

Linux packages

This section is devoted to managing software packages under Linux. It will cover the day-to-day handling of basic utilities such as dpkg and rpm, as well as repository managers such as apt and yum. We will extend this view with other tools such as opkg, pacman, emerge or apk.

4.3.1. Package manager

4.3.1.1. Package manager

A package manager is one or more tools that automate the process of installing, uninstalling and updating software installed on a computer system.

A package is an archive containing the computer files, information and procedures needed to install software on an operating system, ensuring the functional consistency of the modified system.

4.3.1.2. Usefulness

The package manager allows you to perform various operations on the packages available:

- Installing, updating and uninstalling ;
- Use of packages from various media (installation CDs, Internet downloads, network shares, etc.);
- Checking the checksums of each recovered packet to verify its integrity ;
- Checking software dependencies to obtain a working version of a package

4.3.1.3. Nomenclature of package systems

There are two main types of package system, depending on the major families of

Linux distributions:

- RPM: Redhat Enterprise Linux, Fedora, Centos, ...
- DPKG: Debian, Ubuntu, Mint, Raspbian, ...

Other systems are also worth considering:

- Port/emerge: Gentoo
- Pacman : Archlinux
- opkg : OpenWRT

4.3.1.4. dpkg utility

Dpkg is used to install, remove and provide information about *deb packages that are supported by Debian-based distributions.

As a low-level tool, dpkg -i / dpkg -r can be used to install or uninstall .deb files. For these tasks, we prefer to use more advanced tools such as aptitude or apt-get, apt-cache.

Useful dpkg commands

To list all packages installed with private rights :

dpkg -l or

dpkg --get-selections

To check that a package is installed :

dpkg -s wget

To list the files installed by a package :

dpkg -L wget

To reconfigure an installed package :

dpkg-reconfigure locales

4.3.1.5. rpm utility

RPM is the other basic system. It allows you to install, update, uninstall, check and search for packages, with root user rights.

To install a package :

rpm -ivh file.rpm

To update a package :

rpm -Uvh file.rpm

To uninstall a package :

rpm -evv file.rpm

Checking the signature of a package :

rpm --checksig file.rpm

rpm -q command

List all installed packages :

rpm -qa

Check that a package is installed :

rpm -q wget

List the files in an installed package :

rpm -ql wget

Get all the information about an installed package :

rpm -qi wget

Obtain all the information about a package before installing it :

rpm -qip file.rpm

4.3.2. Packet depot

An advanced package manager such as apt or yum manages software sources (usually already compiled) and their authenticity.

The place where these sources are placed is called the package repository. This source is usually a local source such as a CD or DVD, an HTTP/FTP Internet server or a local repository mirror.

The definition of a package repository depends not only on the source itself, but also on the distribution, hardware architecture, official sources and other factors.

Some software developers their own installation binaries for distributions and host their own package repositories.

4.3.2.1. Operating principle

How an advanced package manager works :

- The software available is contained in a list that must be kept up to date to ensure consistency throughout the system.
- At the time of the installation request, this list is consulted to select the necessary files.
- The package system decompresses and places the various binary, configuration and documentation files in the appropriate places. Eventually, a configuration dialogue takes place.
- *Eventually*, the package system automatically installs a service and starts it.

Tasks

- Checking the existence of a package
- Software version in the package
- Configuration files
- Source
- /etc configuration files
- Uninstall
- File purging
- Removing orphan dependencies

4.3.2.2. APT

APT simplifies the installation, updating and uninstallation of software by automating the retrieval of packages from APT sources (on the Internet, local network, CD-ROMs, etc.), the management of dependencies and sometimes compilation. When packages are installed, updated or removed, package management programs can display package dependencies, ask the administrator whether packages recommended or suggested by newly installed packages should also be installed, and resolve dependencies automatically. Package management programs can also update all packages.

APT is essentially a C++ library of functions used by several package management programs. One of these programs is apt, probably the best known and the one officially recommended by the Debian project. aptitude is also popular and offers extended functionality compared to apt-get. Today, apt is a command that is sufficient on its own for most operations concerning Debian/Ubuntu packages.

APT sources

The sources from which apt fetches packages are defined in /etc/apt/sources.list

For example, on a Debian 7 Wheezy machine :
cat /etc/apt/sources.list
deb https://http.debian.net/debian wheezy main
deb https://http.debian.net/debian wheezy-updates main
deb https://security.debian.org wheezy/updates main
The **main** section includes all packages which conform to the DFSG - Debian Free Software Guidelines - and which do not require programs outside this scope to function. These are the only packages considered part of the Debian distribution.
The **contrib** section includes all packages which conform to DFSG, but which have dependencies outside main (which can be packaged for Debian in non-free).
The **non-free** section contains software that does not comply with the DFSG.
For example, on an Ubuntu 16.04 Xenial machine :
cat /etc/apt/sources.list
deb https://archive.ubuntu.com/ubuntu xenial main universe
deb https://archive.ubuntu.com/ubuntu xenial-updates main universe
deb https://archive.ubuntu.com/ubuntu xenial-security main universe
Ubuntu officially maintains **main** (free software) packages. software)
and **restricted** (non-free software).
The Ubuntu community provides **universe** (free) and **multiverse** (non-free) packages.
We'll get into the habit of updating the list of packages with :
apt-get update

APT Research

Searching package descriptions :
apt-cache search wget
But apt search also works:
apt search wget
View package information :
apt-cache show wget
Checking the dependencies of a package :
apt-cache showpkg wget

Upgrading and installing with APT

Update all packages without adding new ones :
apt-get update && apt-get upgrade
or :
apt update && apt upgrade
Update all installed packages to the latest versions, installing new packages if necessary:
apt dist-upgrade
Installing or updating a package :
apt install wget
Installation without dialogue :
apt -y install wget

Uninstalling APT packages

Remove packages without configurations :

apt remove wget
Remove packages without dependencies :
apt autoremove wget
Completely remove a package :
apt purge wget
The two can be combined:
apt autoremove --purge wget
Remove unnecessary dependencies :
apt autoremove
Deleting cached files in var/cache/apt/archives :
apt clean
Reinstalling a package :
apt --reinstall install postfix
Installing an "unstable" version :
apt install spamassassin/unstable
apt full-upgrade is also the command used by those who use the Unstable version of Debian on a daily basis and follow its evolutions from day to day. It is so simple that it speaks for itself: it is this functionality that has made APT famous.
aptitude is an interactive program in semi-graphical mode, which can be used on the console browse the list of installed and available packages, view all the information and mark them for installation or removal. Since this time it's a program that's really designed to be used by administrators, it features more intelligent default behaviours than apt-get, as well as a more affordable interface.

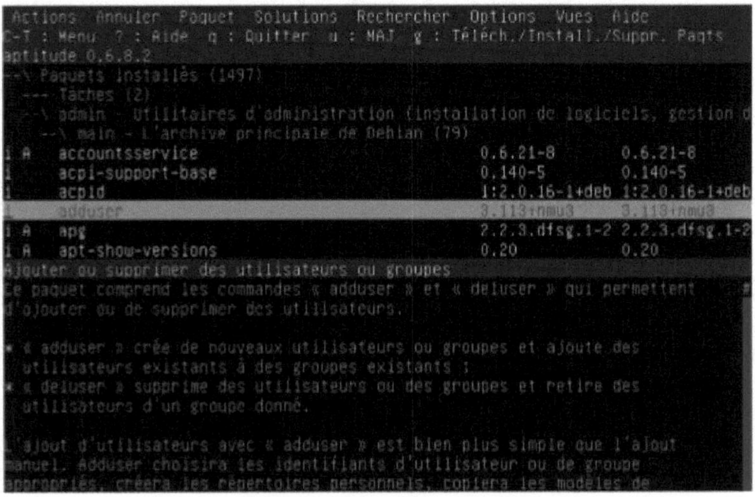

aptitude package manager

synaptic is a Debian package manager in graphical mode (it uses GTK+/GNOME). It has an efficient, clean graphical interface. Its many ready-to-use filters allow you to quickly see what new packages are available, what packages are installed, what packages can be updated, what packages are obsolete, and so on. As you navigate through the various lists, you can progressively indicate the operations to be performed (install, update, remove, purge). A single click is all it takes to validate all these choices, and all the operations recorded are then carried out in a single pass.

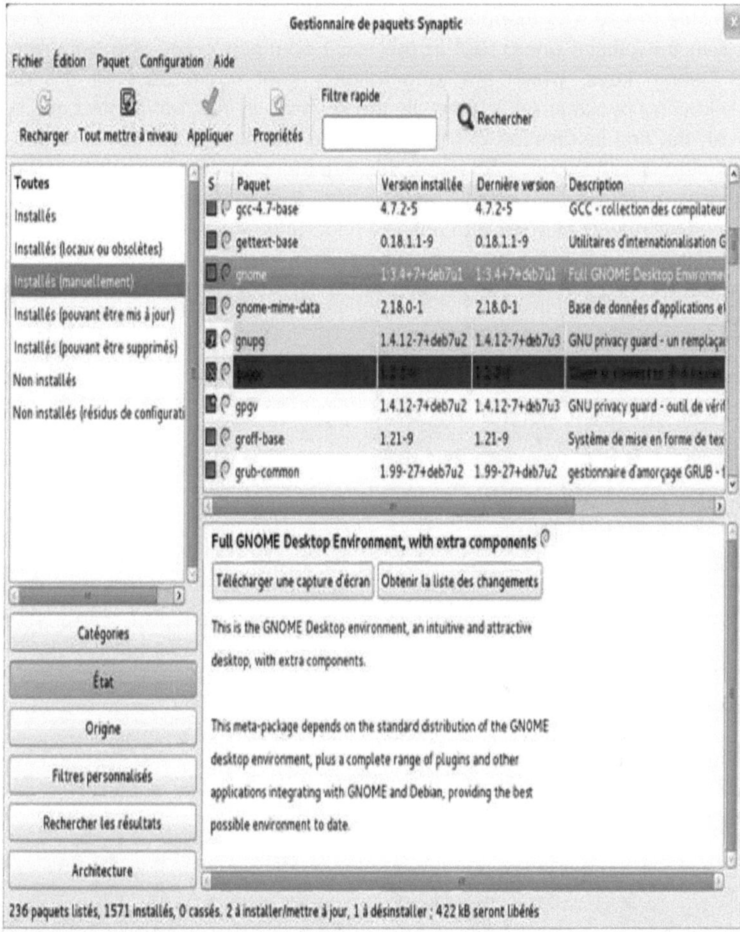

Synaptic package manager

Authentication of Debian packages

Debian offers a way of ensuring that an installed package comes from its maintainer and has not been modified by a third party: there is a package sealing mechanism.

This signature is not direct: the signed file is a Release file placed on the Debian mirrors which lists the various Packages files (including their compressed Packages.gz and Packages.xz forms and incremental versions), along with their MD5, SHA1 and SHA256 checksums (to verify that their contents have not been altered). These Packages files in turn contain a list of Debian packages and their checksums, to ensure that their contents have not been altered either.

Trusted keys are managed using the apt-key program, provided by the apt package. This program maintains a keychain of GnuPG public keys, , which are used to verify the signatures of Release.gpg files obtained from Debian mirrors.
It is possible to use it to manually add additional keys (if you wish to add mirrors other than the official ones); but in the most common case, you only need the official Debian keys, which are automatically kept up to date by the debian-archive-keyring package (which installs the keyrings in '/etc/apt/trusted.gpg.d).
However, the first installation of this package is also questionable, because even if it is signed like the other packages, this signature cannot be verified externally. You should therefore check the fingerprints of the imported keys before trusting them to install new packages with apt-key fingerprint.
For example,

```
apt-key fingerprint
/etc/apt/trusted.gpg.d/debian-archive-jessie-automatic.gpg
-----------------------------------------------------------
pub   4096R/2B90D010 2014-11-21 [expire : 2022-11-19]
 Empreinte de la clef = 126C 0D24 BD8A 2942 CC7D  F8AC 7638 D044 2B90 D010
uid                  Debian Archive Automatic Signing Key (8/jessie)
<ftpmaster@debian.org>

/etc/apt/trusted.gpg.d/debian-archive-jessie-security-automatic.gpg
--------------------------------------------------------------------
pub   4096R/C857C906 2014-11-21 [expire : 2022-11-19]
 Empreinte de la clef = D211 6914 1CEC D440 F2EB  8DDA 9D6D 8F6B C857 C906
uid                  Debian Security Archive Automatic Signing Key (8/jessie)
<ftpmaster@debian.org>

/etc/apt/trusted.gpg.d/debian-archive-jessie-stable.gpg
-------------------------------------------------------
pub   4096R/518E17E1 2013-08-17 [expire : 2021-08-15]
 Empreinte de la clef = 75DD C3C4 A499 F1A1 8CB5  F3C8 CBF8 D6FD 518E 17E1
uid                  Jessie Stable Release Key <debian-release@lists.debian.org>

/etc/apt/trusted.gpg.d/debian-archive-squeeze-automatic.gpg
-----------------------------------------------------------
pub   4096R/473041FA 2010-08-27 [expire : 2018-03-05]
 Empreinte de la clef = 9FED 2BCB DCD2 9CDF 7626  78CB AED4 B06F 4730 41FA
uid                  Debian Archive Automatic Signing Key (6.0/squeeze)
<ftpmaster@debian.org>
```

```
/etc/apt/trusted.gpg.d/debian-archive-squeeze-stable.gpg
--------------------------------------------------------
pub   4096R/B98321F9 2010-08-07 [expire : 2017-08-05]
 Empreinte de la clef = 0E4E DE2C 7F3E 1FC0 D033  800E 6448 1591 B983 21F9
uid                  Squeeze Stable Release Key <debian-release@lists.debian.org>

/etc/apt/trusted.gpg.d/debian-archive-wheezy-automatic.gpg
----------------------------------------------------------
pub   4096R/46925553 2012-04-27 [expire : 2020-04-25]
 Empreinte de la clef = A1BD 8E9D 78F7 FE5C 3E65  D8AF 8B48 AD62 4692 5553
uid                  Debian Archive Automatic Signing Key (7.0/wheezy)
<ftpmaster@debian.org>

/etc/apt/trusted.gpg.d/debian-archive-wheezy-stable.gpg
-------------------------------------------------------
pub   4096R/65FFB764 2012-05-08 [expire : 2019-05-07]
 Empreinte de la clef = ED6D 6527 1AAC F0FF 15D1  2303 6FB2 A1C2 65FF B764
uid                  Wheezy Stable Release Key <debian-release@lists.debian.org>
```

Prevent a service from starting after an installation

Creating an /usr/sbin/policy-rc.d exit script will prevent the service from being launched after installation.

```
cat > /usr/sbin/policy-rc.d << EOF
#!/bin/sh
echo "All runlevel operations denied by policy" >&2
exit 101
EOF
chmod +x /usr/sbin/policy-rc.d
```

existence of this script will give this message after an installation:

```
All runlevel operations denied by policy
invoke-rc.d: policy-rc.d denied execution of start.
```

1.1.1.3. YUM / DNF

"Yum", for "Yellowdog Updater Modified", is a package manager for Linux distributions such as Fedora and Red Hat Enterprise Linux, created by Yellow Dog Linux.

"Dandified Yum" or "DNF" is the successor to YUM, which been used almost identically since Red Hat Enterprise Linux 8 and Fedora 22.

YUM and DNF are used manage the installation and updating of software installed on a Red Hat-type distribution. They are RPM overlays that manage downloads and dependencies, in the same way as Debian's APT.

YUM basic commands

Unlike APT, YUM updates its list of packages automatically.

Search for a package :

```
yum search wget
```

List information about a package :

```
yum list wget
yum info wget
```

Installing a package :

```
yum install wget
```

Install a package without dialogue:

```
yum -y install wget
```

Uninstalling a package

```
yum remove wget
```

YUM update

Updating a :

```
yum update wget
```

Check available updates :

```
yum check-update
```

Security and binary updates :

```
yum update
```

YUM Group Packages

Package groups are collections of packages:

```
yum groups list
yum groups info group
yum groups install group
yum groups update group
yum groups remove group
```

YUM package repositories

List of package repositories :

```
yum repolist
yum repolist all
```

Install an additional EPEL (Extra Packages for Enterprise Linux) repository :

```
yum install epel-release
```

Install an additional repository

The repository configuration is located in the /etc/yum.repos.d/ folder:

```
ls /etc/yum.repos.d/
CentOS-Base.repo  CentOS-Debuginfo.repo  CentOS-Media.repo    CentOS-
Vault.repo
CentOS-CR.repo    CentOS-fasttrack.repo  CentOS-Sources.repo
```

For example, the first repository configured in the CentOS-Base.repo file :

```
[base]
name=CentOS-$releasever - Base
mirrorlist=https://mirrorlist.centos.org/?release=$releasever&arch=$basearch&repo=
os&infra=$infra
#baseurl=https://mirror.centos.org/centos/$releasever/os/$basearch/
gpgcheck=1
gpgkey=file:///etc/pki/rpm-gpg/RPM-GPG-KEY-CentOS-7
```

There is a section declaration [base] in the header and four essential variables

- name which indicates the name of the repository.
- mirrorlist or baseurl, which indicate the location of the repository
- gpgckeck which requests an integrity check and gpgkey which sets the check file. It is not necessary for gpckeck=0 to be configured.
- Finally, enabled=1 would enable the repository to be taken into account.

The yum-config-manager utility makes it easy to add a repository:

```
yum-config-manager --add-repo=https://ftp.belnet.be/ftp.centos.org/7/os/x86_64/
Modules complémentaires chargés : fastestmirror, langpacks
adding repo from: https://ftp.belnet.be/ftp.centos.org/7/os/x86_64/

[ftp.belnet.be_ftp.centos.org_7_os_x86_64_]
name=added from: https://ftp.belnet.be/ftp.centos.org/7/os/x86_64/
baseurl=https://ftp.belnet.be/ftp.centos.org/7/os/x86_64/
enabled=1
```

Add gpgcheck=0 :

```
echo "gpgcheck=0" >>
/etc/yum.repos.d/ftp.belnet.be_ftp.centos.org_7_os_x86_64_.repo
cat /etc/yum.repos.d/ftp.belnet.be_ftp.centos.org_7_os_x86_64_.repo
[ftp.belnet.be_ftp.centos.org_7_os_x86_64_]
name=added from: https://ftp.belnet.be/ftp.centos.org/7/os/x86_64/
baseurl=https://ftp.belnet.be/ftp.centos.org/7/os/x86_64/
enabled=1

gpgcheck=0
```

Update the list of packages :

```
yum clean all
yum repolist
```

YUM package management

List installed packages :

```
yum list installed | less
```

Clear the /var/cache/yum/ cache:

```
yum clean all
```

History of yum transactions:

```
yum history
```

1.1.1.4. Other package management software

- Pacman: Arch Linux.
- Emerging: Gentoo
- Opkg : Openwrt

4.3.3. Maintenance and updates

4.3.3.1. Maintaining updates for a Debian system

apticron, in the package of the same name. This is simply a script, called daily by cron, which updates the list of available packages and sends an e-mail a given address listing the packages that are not installed in their latest version, along a description of the changes that have taken place. This script is mainly aimed at Debian Stable users, as you'd expect.

We can therefore take advantage of the /etc/cron.daily/apt script, installed by the apt package. This script is also run daily by cron, so there is no interactive interface. To control its operation, we'll use APT configuration variables (which will be stored in a file under /etc/apt/apt.conf.d/). The most important are :

- APT :: Periodic::Update-Package-Lists
- APT :: Periodic ::Download-Upgradeable-Packages
- APT :: Periodic::AutocleanInterval
- APT :: Periodic ::Unattended-Upgrade

```
APT::Periodic::Update-Package-Lists
```

This option allows you to specify a frequency (in days) for updating package lists. If you are using apticron, you can without it, as it would be duplicating efforts.

```
APT::Periodic::Download-Upgradeable-Packages
```

This option also specifies a frequency in days for downloading updated packages. Here again, apticron users can do without it.

```
APT::Periodic::AutocleanInterval
```

This option covers a function that apticron does not have: it specifies the frequency at which the APT cache can be automatically purged of obsolete packages (those that are no longer available on mirrors or referenced by any distribution). This means you don't have to worry about the size of the APT cache, which will be automatically regulated.

```
APT::Periodic::Unattended-Upgrade
```

When this option is enabled, the daily script will run unattended-upgrade (in the unattended-upgrades package) which, as its name suggests, automates the upgrade process for certain packages; by default, it only handles security upgrades, but this is configurable in the /etc/apt/apt.conf.d/50unattended-upgrades file). Note that this option can be enabled with debconf, using the command dpkg-reconfigure -plow unattended-upgrades.

4.3.3.2. Upgrading a Debian distribution from an older version

Upgrading from Debian 7 (wheezy) to Debian 8 (jessie)

Recommendations :

- Delete unnecessary packages
- Updating the current system
- Backing up data

Updating the Debian Wheezy distribution :

```
apt-get update
apt-get upgrade
apt-get dist-upgrade
```

Update installation sources :

```
sed -i 's/wheezy/jessie/g' /etc/apt/sources.list
```

Updating packages :

```
apt-get update
apt-get -y upgrade
```

Update distribution :

```
apt-get -y dist-upgrade
```

Restart:

```
reboot
```

Check the version:

```
hostnamectl
  Static hostname: wheezy1
        Icon name: computer-vm
          Chassis: vm
       Machine ID: cab21b38a8058c4d3f6641f1587fa5b7
          Boot ID: cde0bd1e7ada4c44acd12bae10adff75
   Virtualization: kvm
 Operating System: Debian GNU/Linux 8 (jessie)
           Kernel: Linux 3.16.0-4-amd64
     Architecture: x86-64
```

Update :

```
apt-get update
apt-get -y upgrade
```

```
apt-get -y autoremove
apt-get -y dist-upgrade
```

Upgrading from Debian 8 (jessie) to Debian 9 (stretch)

The procedure is identical from Debian 8 Jessie to Debian 9 Stretch.

```
cp /etc/apt/sources.list /etc/apt/sources.list_backup
sed -i 's/jessie/stretch/g' /etc/apt/sources.list
apt-get update
apt-get -y upgrade
apt-get -y dist-upgrade
reboot
apt-get update
apt-get -y upgrade
apt-get -y autoremove
apt-get -y dist-upgrade
hostnamectl
  Static hostname: wheezy1
        Icon name: computer-vm
          Chassis: vm
       Machine ID: cab21b38a8058c4d3f6641f1587fa5b7
          Boot ID: efd16e22f98a42d0a7d3cf44dba21fc9
   Virtualization: kvm
 Operating System: Debian GNU/Linux 9 (stretch)
           Kernel: Linux 4.8.0-2-amd64
     Architecture: x86-64
```

Ubuntu version updates

Source : https://doc.ubuntu-fr.org/migration

Highly inadvisable, the procedure suggests moving from revision to revision. A system backup is then recommended.

The do-release-upgrade command-line tool lets you upgrade Ubuntu without using a graphical utility. It is particularly relevant for servers, which operate without a graphical interface. All the options in this tool can be read by running the command :

```
do-release-upgrade –help
```

Here are some of the most useful options:

```
do-release-upgrade –check-dist-upgrade-only
```

The -check-dist-upgrade-only option checks the existence a new version. If a new version is found, the result is displayed in the terminal. Executed in this way, this command only performs a check; upgrade is performed.

```
do-release-upgrade –sandbox
```

The -sandbox option can be used to test an upgrade in a protected environment. This is particularly useful for testing the deployment of an upgrade before applying it in the production environment.

```
do-release-upgrade
```

Without an option, the do-release-upgrade tool searches for and upgrades to the next available LTS or stable version, if one exists.

4.3.4. Comparison of package managers by distribution

From the point of view of the system administrator, Linux distributions *can* be distinguished by :

1. the package manager and system
2. initialisation scripts and execution levels
3. the starter charger
4. the location of network configuration files and repositories

The focus here is on "genetic" differences packet management.

4.3.4.1. Debian/Ubuntu v. Fedora/RHEL/SL/Centos

Action	Debian/Ubuntu	Fedora/RHEL/SL/Centos
1. Updating the list of packages	apt-get update	yum update, yum check-update
2. Display of available updates	apt-get upgrade -simulate	yum list updates
3. Installing specific packages	apt-get install packagel package2	yum install packagel package2
4. Reinstalling a package	apt-get install --reinstall package	yum reinstall package
5. Updating a package	apt-get upgrade packagel package2	yum update package
6. Updating the system	apt-get upgrade, apt-get dist-upgrade, apt upgrade, apt full-upgrade	yum upgrade

Action	Debian/Ubuntu	Fedora/RHEL/SL/Centos
7. Packet search	apt-cache search searchword, apt-cache search --full --names-only searchword	yum search searchword
8. List of installed packages	dpkg -1, apt list --installed	rpm -qa
9. Package information	apt-cache show package, apt show package, dpkg -s package	yum info package, yum list package, yum deplist package
10. Uninstalling packages	apt-get remove --purge packagel package2, apt-get autoremove	yum remove packagel package2
11. Downloading packages without installation	apt-get install --download-only packagel package2	yum install --downloadonly --downloaddir=<directory> <package>
12. Clear downloaded packets	apt-get clean, apt-get clean (outdated packages)	yum clean all
13. Repository configuration	/etc/apt/sources.list	/etc/yum.repos.d/

4.3.4.2. Alpine Linux v. Arch Linux v. Gentoo

Action	Alpine Linux	Arch Linux	Gentoo
1. Updating the list of packages	apk update	pacman -Sy	emerge -sync
2. Display of available updates	apk version -v or apk version -V -1 '<'	pacman -Qu	emerge -Dupv world or emerge --deep - -update --pretend world
3. Installing specific packages	apk add packagel package2	pacman -S packagel package2	emerge packagel package2
4. Reinstalling a package	apk del packagel && apk add packagel	pacman -Sf packagel package2	emerge --oneshot packagel
5. Updating a package	apk add -u packagel	pacman -S packagel	emerge --update packagel package2

	package2	package2		

Action	Alpine Linux	Arch Linux	Gentoo	
6. Updating the system	-	pacman -Syu	-	
7. Packet search	apk search searchword	pacman -Ss searchword, pacma n -Si packagenam e	emerge --searchdesc searchword, eix searchword, esearch searchword	yum search searchwo r d
8. List of installed packages	apk info	pacman - Qs, pacman - Q, pacman -Q	emerge gentoolkit && equery list	
9. Package information	apk info -a package	pacman -Si package	-	
10. Uninstalling packages	apk del packagel package2	pacman -R packagel package2	emerge --depclean packagel package2	
11. Download	apk fetch packagel package2	pacman -Sw packagel package2	emerge --fetchonly packagel package2	
Action	**Alpine Linux**	**Arch Linux**	**Gentoo**	
t packages without installation				
12. Deleting downloaded packages	*Automatic*	*Automatic*	rm -rf /usr/portage/distfiles/*	
13. Repository configuratio n	/etc/apk/repositori e s	/etc/opkg.con f	etc/portage/repos.conf/gentoo.con f, э t much more	

4.3.4.3. OpenWRT

Action	OpenWRT
1. Updating the list of packages	opkg update
2. Display of available updates	opkg list-upgradable
3. Installing specific packages	opkg install <pkgs or FQDN>
Action	**OpenWRT**
4. Reinstalling a package	opkg install --force-reinstall <pkgs>
5. Updating a package	opkg upgrade <pkgs> (not recommended)
6. Updating the system	opkg upgrade
7. Packet search	opkg list [pkg or globp],opkg search <file or globp>
8. List of installed packages	opkg list-installed
9. Package information	opkg info [pkg or globp],opkg status [pkg or

	globp].
10. Uninstalling packages	opkg remove <pkgs or globp>
11. Downloading packages without installation	opkg --download-only download <pkg>
12. Deleting downloaded packages	option - -force-removal-of-dependent-packages
13. Repository configuration	/etc/opkg.conf

4.3.5. Update the kernel

4.3.5.1. RHEL procedure

```
yum update kernel
```

or if the rpm file is available

```
rpm -ivh kernel.rpm
```

The last kernel installed becomes the default kernel:

```
grub2-editenv list
saved_entry=CentOS Linux (3.10.0-327.13.1.el7.x86_64) 7 (Core)
grep ^menuentry /boot/grub2/grub.cfg
menuentry 'CentOS Linux (3.10.0-327.13.1.el7.x86_64) 7 (Core)' --class centos --class gnu-linux --class gnu --class os --unrestricted $menuentry_id_option 'gnulinux-3.10.0-327.el7.x86_64-advanced-5cc65046-7a0e-450b-99e8-f0cc34954d75' {
menuentry 'CentOS Linux (3.10.0-327.el7.x86_64) 7 (Core)' --class centos --class gnu-linux --class gnu --class os --unrestricted $menuentry_id_option 'gnulinux-3.10.0-327.el7.x86_64-advanced-5cc65046-7a0e-450b-99e8-f0cc34954d75' {
menuentry 'CentOS Linux (0-rescue-d939e80ee5d6473297b10a3839c85928) 7 (Core)' --class centos --class gnu-linux --class gnu --class os --unrestricted $menuentry_id_option 'gnulinux-0-rescue-d939e80ee5d6473297b10a3839c85928-advanced-5cc65046-7a0e-450b-99e8-f0cc34954d75' {
```

Modify the default kernel :

```
grub2-set-default 0
```

Generate configuration :

```
grub2-mkconfig -o /boot/grub2/grub.cfg
Generating grub configuration file ...
Found linux image: /boot/vmlinuz-3.10.0-327.13.1.el7.x86_64
Found initrd image: /boot/initramfs-3.10.0-327.13.1.el7.x86_64.img
Found linux image: /boot/vmlinuz-3.10.0-327.el7.x86_64
Found initrd image: /boot/initramfs-3.10.0-327.el7.x86_64.img
Found linux image: /boot/vmlinuz-0-rescue-d939e80ee5d6473297b10a3839c85928
Found initrd image: /boot/initramfs-0-rescue-d939e80ee5d6473297b10a3839c85928.img
done
```

4.3.5.2. Ubuntu procedure

Here's how to install **Ubuntu** on your computer:

1. **Prerequisites** :

○ Check that your computer meets the minimum requirements:

■ **Office version** :

■ 2 GHz processor

■ 4 GB RAM

■ 8 GB hard disk space (25 GB recommended)

■ Graphics card with 1024x768 resolution

■ **Server version** :

■ 1 GHz processor

■ 1 GB RAM

■ 2.5 GB hard disk space

○ Make sure that your computer can access the BIOS or boot from an external device (except in specific cases such as the Raspberry Pi).

○ Download **Ubuntu** from the download page.

2. **Create an installation USB key** :

○ Use a USB key of at least 6 GB.

○ You can use tools such as **Unetbootin** to create the bootable USB key.

3. **Installing Ubuntu** :

○ Insert the USB key into your computer.

○ Restart the computer and select the USB key as the boot device.

○ Follow the on-screen instructions to install Ubuntu.

Installing Ubuntu

Prerequisites

Choice of architecture

Ubuntu is available for a wide range of architectures (determined by the hardware): officially, computers based on x64 (64-bit) processors are supported, but unofficially, Ubuntu also supports PowerPC, HPPA, ia64 and SPARC.

Most new commercial computers are compatible with the **64-bit** version.

System requirements depending on the variant.

1. **Office version:**

Details in English: https://help.ubuntu.com/community/Installation/SystemRequirements

○ 2 GHz processor

○ 4 GB RAM

- 8 GB hard disk space (25 GB recommended)
- A graphics card with a resolution 1024x768

2. **Server version:** 2)

Details in English: https://ubuntu.com/server/docs/installation

- 1 GHz processor
- 1 GB RAM
- 2.5 GB hard disk space.

Your computer must also allow you to access the BIOS or at least boot from external media (except in specific cases using particular versions of Ubuntu, such as for the Raspberry Pi).

Choice of support

Ubuntu and its variants are available on the *Download* page (see also the *Installation* section of this page).

It is generally recommended that you install it from a USB stick. You can *flash* any key of at least 6 GB (some variants fit on smaller keys - the size of the images is displayed by hovering over the *Download* buttons).

- Live-USB: **Use and install Ubuntu from a USB stick**.
- Installation from CD see **Standard installation with the Ubuntu CD**
- Other media: see Special cases

If you are using Windows

To prepare for your migration from Windows to Ubuntu: to find out all the differences, and how to resolve certain incompatibility problems between these two worlds, consult this documentation on Windows.

Upgrading to a later version

Upgrading to a higher version Ubuntu does not require a complete reinstall of your system. Ubuntu can be upgraded directly from the Internet or from Ubuntu installation media, using the upgrade utility.

- Upgrade without Internet : if you want to upgrade your version *via* a prepared removable disk.
- To upgrade your version from the Internet, a USB stick or a CD/DVD, see the Migrating to a later version page.

Changing Ubuntu variants without reinstalling

It is possible to change Ubuntu variants without reinstalling the system. Using this method, you can also install (as it were) two Ubuntu variants at the same time (you can choose the environment in your connection window):

- Switch to Kubuntu
- Switch to Xubuntu
- Switch to Lubuntu
- Switching to Ubuntu (Unity)

Reinstalling Ubuntu without losing your data

If you're reinstalling Ubuntu completely, here's how to keep your /home (the folder containing your personal files and software configuration and interface): see the Ubuntu Reinstallation tutorial.

Repeating an installation

You can create a custom CD and use it for several installations.

Multi-boot: Ubuntu and Windows, OS (or other) on the same computer

• Install Ubuntu alongside Windows, OS (or others) (dual-boot).

Special cases

Via the ISO image without using a CD drive :

• Live-USB: **Install Ubuntu on (or via) a USB stick** with or without data persistence.

o Install Ubuntu with Unetbootin. Install Ubuntu directly from an ISO image stored on a hard drive or USB key (if you have Internet access and no CD drive, for example).

o Install Ubuntu without a CD: install Ubuntu from an ISO image on a hard disk or USB key (or from Internet repositories), without burning a CD.

• Via the network :

o Installation from another computer (network computer). The computer must be able to boot via the network (e.g. PXE), and *another computer* must act as the image server on the network. This method is fairly complex to set up the first time, but much simpler for subsequent installations, if there are *several computers to install* and for *customising installations*.

o Installation when you can't boot from the CD-ROM and the computer boots from the network (e.g. PXE)

o Install Ubuntu over the Internet: a ~13MB ISO that downloads and installs Ubuntu over the Internet

• Installation on secondary media :

o On a USB hard disk: classic installation, but on a USB disk ;

o See also Live-USB to use a USB stick with persistent boot, so it can be used from any PC;

• Alternative installation methods :

o Installation when you cannot boot from CD-ROM but have a floppy drive;

• Other methods for less powerful computers :

o Install the bare essentials to get a clean desktop, without all the unnecessary software installed by default;

If your screen is broken

If your laptop's screen is broken, simply plug in another screen with a VGA or HDMI cable, and launch the installation in the usual way.

4.4. Security and backup management

Linux is an open source operating system based on the kernel of the Unix operating system. It is widely used in web servers, supercomputers, smartphones and desktops. Linux is known for being stable, efficient and secure.

Linux is also very popular as a development operating system, as it offers full access to source code and great customisation flexibility. Many developers also appreciate the active community of Linux developers and users, who provide help and advice online.

Why is Linux considered secure?

There are several reasons why Linux is considered secure:

• . **Managing users and groups** : Linux allows you to create several users and groups with different levels of access rights. This makes it possible to restrict access to sensitive files and commands to unauthorised users.

- . **Managing access rights and permissions** : Linux lets you define very granular access rights and permissions on files and directories. This prevents unauthorised users from accessing or modifying sensitive files.
- . **Automatic updating of software and security patches**: Linux offers automatic updating of software and security patches, protecting the system against known vulnerabilities.
- . **Active community of developers and users**: Linux has an active community of developers and users who work together to identify and correct system vulnerabilities. This helps to keep the system secure.
- . **Low virus rate**: due to its limited popularity as a desktop operating system, Linux has a low virus rate compared to other operating systems (Windows and Mac OS). This means that it y less likely to be contaminated by viruses or malicious software.

What is the most secure Linux distribution?

It is difficult to determine which Linux distribution is the most secure, as security depends on many factors, such as system configuration, installed software and security practices in place.

However, some Linux distributions are considered to be more secure than others, because special attention has been paid to security in their design and maintenance.

Using a commercial distribution, i.e. one that has to be paid for, often provides additional security guarantees for servers. However, some community distributions, i.e. free distributions, are renowned for their reliability and security.

Here are the free Linux distributions that are considered to offer a high level of security for servers:

- **Debian**: this Linux distribution is very popular with developers. It is one of the most stable and secure distributions.
- **Fedora**: community distribution of Red Hat Enterprise Linux. It incorporates additional tools to enhance security.
- **OpenSUSE**: community distribution SUSE, it is easy to use, reliable and secure.

For desktop computers, here are the distributions that offer enhanced security: Kodachi, Qubes, Whonix, Tails, Discret, IprediaOS and Dizaines (Tens).

It is important to note that the security of any Linux distribution depends on how it is configured and used. Even the most secure distributions can be compromised if they are poorly configured or if good security practices are not followed.

There are distributions designed to test the vulnerability of servers, networks and computer systems. The main ones are : Kali, Parrot and BlackArch. These distributions are equipped tools for carrying out attacks to test the security of your own systems.

How to secure a Linux server

Managing users and groups

User and group management is an important security measure to protect a Linux server[12] . It allows you to control who has access to which functions and files on

---

[12] Richard Stevens, "Advanced Programming in the UNIX Environment" - Addison-Wesley

the server.

To manage users and groups on a Linux server, you can use the following commands :

- useradd: used to create a new user.
- passwd: used to set or change a user's password.
- usermod: used to modify a user's details, for example their name or main group.
- groupadd: used to create a new group.
- userdel: deletes a user.
- groupdel: used to delete a group.

It is advisable to create users and groups with explicit names and to give them limited access rights to the files and commands they need to carry out their work. This minimises the risk of unauthorised leaks or modifications sensitive data.

It is also advisable to change user passwords regularly and make them strong and unique to prevent brute force attacks.

Managing access rights and permissions

Managing access rights and permissions is another important security measure for protecting a Linux server. It allows you to control who has access to which files and directories on the server, as well as the actions they can perform on these files (read, write, execute).

To manage access rights and permissions on a Linux server, you can use the following commands :

- chmod: changes the permissions of a file or directory.
- chown: used to change the owner of a file or directory.
- umask: defines the default permissions for newly created files and directories.

It is advisable to set restrictive permissions on sensitive files and directories, in order to limit access to unauthorised users. For example, you can prohibit certain files from being written to or executed by users who do not need these functions.

It is also advisable to define the owner and main group of a file or directory appropriately, in order to control who has access to these resources.

You can restrict access to certain sensitive commands and functions on your Linux server using user and group management and access rights and permissions management.

To do this, you need to use the sudo command to give certain users access to certain sensitive commands and functions, while restricting access to other users. To use sudo, you must first add the user to the list of authorised users in the /etc/sudoers file.

Automatic software and security patch updates

Automatic updating of software and security patches is an important feature of Linux, helping to protect the system against known vulnerabilities.

To automatically update software and security patches on a Linux server, you can use the following commands:

- apt-get update: updates the list of packages available in the repositories.
- apt-get upgrade: upgrades all installed packages to more recent versions.

Professional, 2013.

• apt-get dist-upgrade: updates all installed packages, including distribution upgrades (for example, upgrading to a new version of Ubuntu).

It is recommended that you regularly update the software and security patches on your Linux server, in order to protect the system against known vulnerabilities. This can be done automatically using a package management tool such as apt-get, or by manually downloading and installing available updates.

It is also advisable to set up a notification system so that you are informed when new updates are available. This way, you can react quickly and update the system before it is compromised.

Use a firewall

A firewall is software or hardware that controls access to your server by allowing or blocking incoming and outgoing connections. You can use a firewall such as iptables or ufw to protect your server against external attacks.

To install a firewall on a Linux server, you can use the iptables tool, which is included in most Linux distributions. Here are the steps to follow:

Check that iptables is installed on your server:

```
apt-get install iptables
```

Create a firewall rule to block all unauthorised incoming connections:

```
iptables -A INPUT -j DROP
```

Allow incoming connections on the necessary ports, such as 80 (HTTP) and 22 (SSH) :

```
iptables -A INPUT -p tcp --dport 80 -j ACCEPT
iptables -A INPUT -p tcp --dport 22 -j ACCEPT
```

Save firewall rules :

```
iptables-save > /etc/iptables/rules.v4
```

Load firewall rules at startup :

```
echo "iptables-restore < /etc/iptables/rules.v4" >> /etc/rc.local
```

You can also use the ufw (Uncomplicated Firewall) tool to easily configure and manage a firewall on your Linux server.

A fundamental principle of security is to open only the ports you need.

Installing an antivirus

Although viruses are less common on Linux than on other operating systems , it is still advisable to install an antivirus to protect your server against malicious software. You can use antivirus software such as ClamAV or Sophos on your Linux server.

To install an antivirus on a Linux server, you can use the ClamAV tool, which is a popular open source antivirus. Here are the steps to follow:

Check that ClamAV is installed on your server:

```
apt-get install clamav
```

Update the virus database:

```
freshclam
```

Scan your system viruses:

```
clamscan -r /
```

This command will recursively scan all files on your system viruses. If viruses are detected, they will be displayed in the command output.

You can also use Sophos to protect your Linux server against viruses and malware. Sophos is a paid-for antivirus solution that offers advanced protection against online threats.

Encrypting disks and files

Disk and file encryption protects sensitive data on your server by making it unreadable to unauthorised users. You can use tools such as LUKS or dm-crypt to encrypt your server's disks, and tools such as GnuPG or OpenSSL to encrypt files.

To encrypt the disks on a Linux server, you can use the LUKS (Linux Unified Key Setup) tool. Here are the steps to follow:

Install LUKS on your server:

```
apt-get install cryptsetup
```

Create an encrypted volume on the disk to be encrypted:

```
cryptsetup -y -v luksFormat /dev/sda1
```

Open the encrypted volume:

```
cryptsetup luksOpen /dev/sda1 sda1_crypt
```

Format the encrypted volume:

```
mkfs.ext4 /dev/mapper/sda1_crypt
```

Create a directory to mount the encrypted volume:

```
mkdir /mnt/encrypted
```

Mount the encrypted volume:

```
mount /dev/mapper/sda1_crypt /mnt/encrypted
```

To decrypt the disk, use the "umount" command to unmount the volume, then use the "cryptsetup luksClose sda1_crypt" command to close the encrypted volume.

To encrypt individual files on your Linux server, you can use the GnuPG (GNU Privacy Guard) tool. Here are the steps to follow:

Install GnuPG on your server:

```
apt-get install gnupg
```

Create an encryption key :

```
gpg --full-generate-key
```

Select the "RSA and RSA (default)" option and enter the information requested, such as name and email address.

Encrypt the file using the encryption key :

```
gpg -c myfile.txt
```

This will create an encrypted file named myfile.txt.gpg.

To decrypt the file, use the following command:

```
gpg myfile.txt.gpg
```

This will create a decrypted file named myfile.txt.

You can also use the OpenSSL tool to encrypt and decrypt files on your Linux server. See the OpenSSL documentation for more information on using this tool.

Make regular back-ups

It is important to create regular backups of your data so that you can restore it if it is lost or corrupted. You can use tools such as rsync or tar to create backups of your data on your Linux server.

Here are the steps to follow to make regular backups with the rsync tool:

Install rsync on your server:

```
apt-get install rsync
```

Create a destination directory for the backups:

```
mkdir /mnt/backup
```

Run the rsync command to make a backup of the :

```
rsync -avz /home/ /mnt/backup
```

This command recursively copies all the files in /home/ to the /mnt/backup .

To automate backups, you can use a task scheduling tool such as cron.

You can also use the tar tool to create archives of your backups and compress them to save disk space.

Make sure you store backups in a secure location and test them regularly to ensure they are valid.

Use strong, unique passwords

It is important to use strong, unique passwords to protect your accounts and data on your Linux server. You can use a password manager such as LastPass or KeePass to generate and manage strong, unique passwords.

Using a virtual private network (VPN)

A VPN encrypts the data passing between your server and the clients accessing it, protecting against spying and data interception. You can use VPN software such as OpenVPN or WireGuard on your Linux server.

Chapter 5

Unix/Linux programming

5.1. Using system libraries

In this chapter, we are going to talk about *shared libraries,* also known as *shared* objects: compiled, reusable bits of code such as functions or classes that are used repeatedly by different programs.
To start with, we'll explain what shared libraries are, how to identify them and where to find them. Next, we'll look at how to configure their storage locations. Finally, we'll show you how to find the shared libraries on which a particular program depends.

The concept of shared libraries

Like their hardware counterparts, software libraries are collections of code intended to be used by many different programs; just as physical libraries hold books and other resources that can be used by many different people.
To build an executable file from the source code of a program, two important steps are necessary. Firstly, the *compiler* transforms the source code into machine code, which is stored in so-called *object files*. Next, the *linker* combines the object files and *links* them to the libraries to generate the final executable file. Linking can be done either *statically* or *dynamically*. Depending on the method chosen, we will talk about static libraries or, in the case of dynamic link editing, shared libraries. Let's explain the differences.

Static libraries

A static library is integrated into the program when the link is created. A copy of the library code is embedded in the program to form part of it. This means that the program does not depend on the library at runtime, as it already contains the library code. The absence of dependencies can be seen as an advantage, as you don't have to worry about the availability of the libraries used. The disadvantage is that statically linked programs are heavier.

Shared (or dynamic) libraries

In the case of shared libraries, the linker simply ensures that the program references the libraries correctly. However, the linker does not copy any code from the library to the program file. At runtime, however, the shared library must be available to satisfy the program's dependencies. This is a cost-effective approach to managing system resources, reducing size of program files by loading only one copy of the library into memory, even if it is used by several programs.

Naming conventions for shared object files

The name of a shared library (*soname*) follows a pattern made up three elements:

- Library name (normally prefixed by lib)
- so (which stands for "shared object")
- Library version number

Here is an example: libpthread.so.0

In comparison, the names of static libraries end in .a, for example libpthread.a.
As files containing shared libraries must be available when
the program is run, most Linux systems contain shared libraries. Since static libraries are only

required in a dedicated file when a program is linked, they may not be present on an end-user system.

The glibc (*GNU C library*) is a good example of a shared library. On a Debian GNU/Linux 9.9 system, its file is named libc.so.6. These rather generic file names are normally symbolic links pointing to the actual file containing a library, whose name contains the exact version number. In the case of glibc, this symbolic link looks like this:

```
$ ls -l /lib/x86_64-linux-gnu/libc.so.6
lrwxrwxrwx 1 root root 12 feb 6 22:17 /lib/x86_64-linux-gnu/libc.so.6 ->
libc-2.24.so
```

This way of referencing shared library files named according to a specific version with more general file names is common practice.

Other examples of shared libraries include `libreadline` (which allows users to edit command lines as they are typed and includes support for Emacs and vi editing modes), `libcrypt` (which contains functions related to encryption, hashing and encoding), or `libcuri` (which is a multi-protocol file transfer library).

Here are the usual locations of shared libraries on a Linux system:

- `/lib`
- `/lib32`
- `/lib64`
- `/usr/lib`
- `/usr/local/lib`

The concept of shared libraries is not specific to Linux. Under Windows, for example, they are called DLLs, which stands for *Dynamic* Link Library.

Configuring shared library paths

References contained in dynamically linked programs are resolved by the dynamic link loader (`id.so` or `id-iinux.so`) when the program is run. The dynamic link loader searches for libraries in a series of directories. These directories are specified by the *library path*. The library path is configured in the `/etc` directory, i.e. in the /etc/ld.so.conf file and, more commonly these days, in the files in the `/etc/id.so.conf.d` directory. Normally, the former includes a single `include` line for the `*.conf` files in the latter:

```
$ cat /etc/ld.so.conf
include /etc/ld.so.conf.d/*.conf
```

The `/etc/id.so.conf`.d directory `contains *.conf` files:

```
$ ls /etc/ld.so.conf.d/
iibc.conf x86_64-iinux-gnu.conf
```

These *.conf files must include the absolute paths to the shared library directories:

```
$ cat /etc/ld.so.conf.d/x86_64-linux-gnu.conf
-   Muitiarch support /iib/x86_64-iinux-gnu /usr/iib/x86_64-iinux-gnu
```

The `idconfig` command reads these configuration files, creates all the symbolic links above to help locate the various libraries and updates the `/etc/id.so`.cache file. This means that `idconfig` must be run each time configuration files are added or updated.

Here are some useful options for `idconfig` :

- `v, -verbose`

Display the version numbers of the libraries, the name of each directory and the links that have been created:

```
$ sudo Idconfig -v
/usr/iocai/iib:
/iib/x86_64-iinux-gnu:
iibnss_myhostname.so.2 -> iibnss_myhostname.so.2 iibfuse.so.2 ->
iibfuse.so.2.9.7
iibidn.so.11 -> iibidn.so.11.6.16
iibnss_mdns4.so.2 -> iibnss_mdns4.so.2 iibparted.so.2 ->
iibparted.so.2.0.1 (...)
```

So, for example, we can see how `iibfuse.so.2` is linked to the effective shared objects file `iibfuse.so.2.9.7`.

- p, -print-cache

Display lists of directories and candidate libraries stored in the current cache :

```
$ sudo Idconfig -p
1094 iibs found in the cache '/etc/id.so.cache'
libzvbi.so.0 (libc6,x86-64) => /usr/iib/x86_64-iinux- gnu/libzvbi.so.0
libzvbi-chains.so.0      (libc6,x86-64)      =>      /usr/iib/x86_64-iinux-
gnu/libzvbi-chains.so.0
libzmq.so.5   (libc6,x86-64)   =>   /usr/lib/x86_64-linux-gnu/libzmq.so.5
libzeitgeist-2.0.so.0 (libc6,x86-64) => /usr/iib/x86_64-iinux-
gnu/libzeitgeist-2.0.so.0
(...)
```

Note how the cache uses the fully qualified *soname* of the links:

```
$ sudo Idconfig -p |grep libfuse
libfuse.so.2 (libc6,x86-64) => /lib/x86_64-linux-gnu/libfuse.so.2
```

If we do a detailed listing of `/lib/x86_64-linux-gnu/libfuse.so.2`, we see the reference to the actual shared object file `iibfuse.so.2.9.7` stored in the same directory :

```
$ Is -l /lib/x86_64-linux-gnu/libfuse.so.2
Irwxrwxrwx 1 root root 16 Aug 21    2018 /lib/x86_64-linux-
gnu/libfuse.so.2 -
> libfuse.so.2.9.7
```

Since you need write access to the `/etc/ld.so`.cache (owned by root), you must either be root or use sudo to invoke `idconfig`. For more information on the `ldconfig` command, see its manual page.

In addition to the configuration files described above, the `LD_LIBRARY_PATH` environment variable can be used to temporarily add new paths for shared libraries. It consists of a

set of directories separated by a colon (:) where the libraries are path. For example, to add `/usr/iocai/myiib` to the library path in the current shell session, you can type :

```
$ LD_LIBRARY_PATH=/usr/local/mylib
```

You can now check its value:

```
$ echo $LD_LIBRARY_PATH
/usr/local/mylib
```

To add `/usr/iocai/myiib` to the library path in the current shell session, exporting it to all child processes created from this shell, type :

```
$ export LD_LIBRARY_PATH=/usr/local/mylib
```

To delete the `LD_LIBRARY_PATH` environment variable, simply type :

```
$ unset LD_LIBRARY_PATH
```

To make the changes permanent, you can write the line

```
export LD_LIBRARY_PATH=/usr/iocai/myiib
```
in one of the Bash initialisation scripts such as `/etc/bash.bashrc` or`~ /.bashrc`. `LD_LIBRARY_PATH` is to shared libraries what `PATH` is to executables. For more information on environment variables and shell configuration, see the relevant lessons.

Search for dependencies on a given executable

To find the shared libraries required by a specific program, use the ldd command followed by the absolute path to the program. The result shows the path to the shared library file and the hexadecimal memory address at which it is loaded:
```
$ ldd /usr/bin/git
linux-vdso.so.1 =>      (0x00007ffcbb310000)
libpcre.so.3 => /lib/x86_64-linux-gnu/libpcre.so.3 (0x00007f18241eb000)
libz.so.1 => /lib/x86_64-linux-gnu/libz.so.1 (0x00007f1823fd1000)
libresolv.so.2 => /lib/x86_64-linux-gnu/libresolv.so.2
(0x00007f1823db6000)
libpthread.so.0 => /lib/x86_64-linux-gnu/libpthread.so.0
(0x00007f1823b99000)
librt.so.1 => /lib/x86_64-linux-gnu/librt.so.1 (0x00007f1823991000)
libc.so.6 => /lib/x86_64-linux-gnu/libc.so.6 (0x00007f18235c7000)
/lib64/ld-linux-x86-64.so.2 (0x00007f182445b000)
```
Similarly, we use ldd to search for dependencies on a shared object:
```
$ ldd /lib/x86_64-linux-gnu/libc.so.6
/lib64/ld-linux-x86-64.so.2 (0x00007fbfed578000) linux-vdso.so.1
(0x00007fffb7bf5000)
```
With the `-u` (or `--unused`) option, `ldd` displays unused direct dependencies (if any):
```
$ ldd -u /usr/bin/git
Unused direct dependencies:
/lib/x86_64-linux-gnu/libz.so.1
/lib/x86_64-linux-gnu/libpthread.so.0 /lib/x86_64-linux-gnu/librt.so.1
```
The presence of unused dependencies is linked to the options used by the linker when building the binary. Even if the program does not need an unused library, it has still been linked and labelled as `NEEDED` in object file information. You can explore this topic using commands such as `readelf` or `objdump`, which you will soon use in in-depth exercise.

The following commands are covered in this lesson:

`ls`

Display the contents of a directory.

`cat`

Concatenate files and display on standard output.

`sudo`

Have a command executed by the super-user with administrator privileges.

`Idconfig`

Configure the link editor's runtime dependencies.

`echo`

Display the value of an environment variable.

`export`

Export the value of an environment variable to child shells.

`unset`

Delete an environment variable.

`ldd`
Display the shared object dependencies of a program.
`readelf`
Display information about ELF files (ELF stands for *executable and linkable format*).
`objdump`
Display information about object files.

Guided exercises

1. Separate the names of the following shared libraries into their components:

Full file name	Library name	suffix *so*	Version number
linux-vdso.so.1			
libprocps.so.6			
libdl.so.2			
libc.so.6			
libsystemd.so.0			
ld-linux-x86-64.so.2			

2. You have developed software and you want to add a new shared library directory to your system (`/opt/iib/myiib`). You write its absolute path in a file called `mylib.conf`.

o In which directory should you store this file?

o What command do you need to run for the changes to take full effect?

3. Which command would you use to list the shared libraries required by `kiii`?

In-depth exercises

1. `objdump` is a command-line tool that displays information about object files. Check whether it is installed on your system with `which objdump`. If not, please install it.

o Use `objdump` with the `p` option (or `- -private-headers`) and `grep` to display the `giibc` dependencies:

o Use `objdump` with the `p` option (or `--private-headers`) and `grep` to display the `giibc` *sonar*.

o Use `objdump` with the `p` option (or `--private-headers`) and `grep` to display Bash dependencies:

In this point, we learned:

- What a shared (or dynamic) library?
- The differences between shared libraries and static libraries.
- The names of shared libraries (*sonames*).
- Preferred locations for shared libraries on a Linux system, such as `/iib` or `/usr/iib`.
- The `id.so` (or `id-iinux.so`) dynamic link editor function.
- How to configure the paths of shared libraries via files in `/etc/` such as `id.so.conf` or those in the `id.so.conf.d` directory.
- How to configure shared library paths using `THE LD_LIBRARY_PATH` environment variable.
- How to search for dependencies on executables and shared libraries.

Answers to guided exercises

1. Separate the names of the following shared libraries into their components:

Full file name	Library name	suffix *so*	Version number
linux-vdso.so.1	linux-vdso	so	1
libprocps.so.6	libprocps	so	6
libdl.so.2	libdl	so	2
libc.so.6	Libc	so	6
iibsystemd.so.0	libsystemd	so	0
ld-linux-x86-64.so.2	ld-linux-x86-64	so	2

2. You have developed software and want to add a new shared library directory to your system (`/opt/iib/myiib`). You write its absolute path in a file called `mylib.conf`.

o In which directory should you store this file?

`/etc/ld.so.conf.d`

o What command do you need to run for the changes to take full effect?

`idconfig`

3. What command would you use to list the shared libraries required by `kiii`?

`idd /bin/kill`

Answers to in-depth exercises

1. `objdump` is a command line tool that displays information about object files. Check if it is installed on your system with `which objdump`. If not, please install it.

o Use `objdump` with the `p` option (or `- -private-headers`) and `grep` to display the `giibc` dependencies:

`objdump -p /lib/x86_64-linux-gnu/libc.so.6 | grep NEEDED`

o Use `objdump` with the `p` option (or `- -private-headers`) and `grep` to display the `giibc` *soname*:

`objdump -p /lib/x86_64-linux-gnu/libc.so.6 | grep SONAME`

o Use `objdump` with the `p` option (or `--private-headers`) and `grep` to display Bash dependencies:

`objdump -p /bin/bash | grep NEEDED`

5.2. Compiling and creating programmes

How do I compile a program under Linux?

In Linux, compiling an application involves starting from the source code, often written in C, to create binaries and libraries. To do this, you use a compiler such as GCC. The sources are retrieved from git or the project website. Sources are generally in the form of files.

To install an application on Linux, you can use the package system of your Linux distribution.

For example, on Debian and Ubuntu, we have **DPKG**.

RPM is the Redhat, CentOS and Fedora package system.

Another method of installing an application on Linux is compilation. This starts with the source code of the application to create binaries and install them in Linux. Thanks to the **gcc (*GNU Compiler Collection*)** compiler, this is possible with any free program.

In this section, we explain why you should compile your applications on Linux. What the advantages are. Why, in some cases, we are obliged to compile an application.

What does it mean to compile programmes from source?

In Linux, compiling an application involves starting from the source code, often written in C, to create binaries and libraries.

To achieve this, we use a **compiler such as GCC**.

We retrieve the sources from git or the project site as described above.

The sources are generally in the form of **.c files and .h files for the headers**.

Then we pass various commands such as **configure, make, make install** to compile and install the binaries in the system.

Why compile programs from source on Linux?

Install utilities not present in the repositories.

Although Linux distribution repositories contain thousands of packages and software, sometimes a piece of software is not present.

This is often the case for projects on Github where the sources are available. In this case, you must compile from source to install and run the software on your system.

Get more recent versions

When you use the package system of a Linux distribution, you may be locked into the versions maintained and offered by the distributions. But sometimes you may need to install a more recent version.

Compiling your own packages will allow you **to obtain highly customised versions** of these packages to better suit your needs. For example, if you install a web server package such as Nginx from the main repository, it will install a pre-configured generic version of Nginx compatible with your distribution.

By compiling Nginx yourself, you can choose which version to install. However, you may not be able to install the very latest version, as the application may rely on system libraries that are too old.

You can find the source code for each version on the free project websites.

Installing customised versions

If you compile Nginx yourself, not only will you be able to compile it with your own configuration flags customised to your particular needs, but you will also be able to enhance it by adding specialised modules such as Google Pagespeed.

During compilation, you **configure the modules to be activated**.

What's more, you can easily add modules that are not supported by your Linux distribution for licensing reasons.

Google's pagespeed module will never be offered by Debian, as it is a proprietary module.

nginx modules on Ubuntu.

As the Ubuntu version is more recent, it offers a few more modules.

By compiling from source, you can activate modules that you don't necessarily have in package form from your Linux distribution's repositories.

Installing an optimised version

Program files are generally created to run on x86-64 compatible computer. However, they can be optimised for a single type of processor, making them faster on that processor.

Without any optimisation options, the compiler's aim is to reduce compilation and ensure that debugging produces the expected results. Setting optimisation flags forces the compiler to try improve performance and/or code size at the expense of compilation time and possibly the ability to debug the program.

The compiler performs an optimisation based on its knowledge of the program. Compiling several files at once into a single output file mode allows the compiler to use the information obtained from all the files when compiling each of them.

During compilation, for best performance, binaries can be optimised using parameters such as CHOST, CFLAGS, CXXFLAGS. GCC also offers options for optimisation starting with -O, such as -O1 ,- O2 or Os.

GCC's -O options also activate optimisation flags.

How do I compile software from Linux sources?

From this link, you can find the basics and commands (configure, make, gcc, etc.) for compiling software from source.

5.3. Debugging and performance optimisation

Linux is an operating system that has won over **hundreds of thousands of users** around the world. It is renowned for its stability, security and flexibility. For those wishing to discover this exciting world, it can be intimidating at first. This sub-point will guide you step-by-step through installing and optimising Linux on your computer, even if you're a beginner.

Choosing the right Linux distribution

There are many Linux distributions, each with its own features and functionality. For a beginner, it is important to choose a distribution that is easy to use, has a large community and good online documentation. Here are some popular options:

- **Ubuntu**: very user-friendly, ideal for beginners.
- **Fedora**: advanced technology, suitable for beginners and experienced users.
- **Archlinux**: customisable, suitable mainly for more advanced users.
- **Debian**: high stability and extensive software catalogue.

Don't hesitate to test several distributions using live USBs before making your final choice.

How do I create a bootable USB flash drive?

The first step is to create a bootable USB key containing the ISO image of the Linux distribution you have chosen. To do this, you'll need bootable USB key creation software such as Etcher or Rufus.

1. Download the ISO image of the distribution you have chosen.
2. Insert your USB key into a USB port on your computer.
3. Open the USB flash drive creation software and select the ISO image and the USB flash drive to be used.
4. Click on "Start" to create the bootable USB key.
5. Restart your computer and access the boot menu (often using F2, F12 or Delete) to select your USB key as the main boot device.

Installing Linux

Once the Linux system has been launched from your bootable USB key, follow the on-screen installation instructions. The steps may vary slightly depending on the distribution you are installing. In general, the processes are as follows:

1. Language selection.
2. Configuring keyboard preferences.

3. Choice of hard drive.
4. Create a user account and password.

In some , you will also need to partition your hard disk manually, but most distributions offer an automatic option to simplify this step.

System update

Once Linux has been installed and booted, one of the first things to do is to update the system to get the latest security and software updates. To do this, open a terminal and enter the following command (the password administrates will be required):

sudo apt-get update && sudo apt-get upgrade

Installation of the necessary graphics drivers

To take full advantage of the performance and functionality of your graphics card under Linux, we recommend that you install the appropriate drivers.

Nvidia

Nvidia cards are generally well supported under Linux. To install Nvidia proprietary drivers (for performance), open a terminal and type :

sudo apt-get install nvidia-driver

Amd/Intel

Amd and Intel cards generally use free drivers called Mesa under Linux. These drivers are already integrated by default into most Linux distributions, and no additional action is required.

System optimisation

Now that Linux is installed and your graphics drivers are configured, here are a few tips for further optimising your system.

Using a package manager

In Linux, a package manager makes it easy to install, configure and remove software on your system. For example, if you use Ubuntu, the package manager is APT (Advanced Package Tool). Here are some useful commands for managing your software:

- sudo apt-get install packageName: installs software
- sudo apt-get remove packageName: uninstalls software
- sudo apt-cache search keyword: searches software based on a keyword

Use official depots and avoid APPs

Repositories are sources that offer software for installation via your package manager. Always use the official repositories for your Linux distribution and avoid unverified third-party repositories wherever possible.

Enable hard disk encryption

To strengthen the security of your system, we recommend that you activate hard disk encryption as soon as you install Linux. This option is often selected when the hard disk is chosen during installation.

Maintain your system regularly

Maintaining your Linux system ensures its stability and optimum performance. Don't forget to make regular back-ups of your important data and to update your system using the package manager.

By following this advice, you'll be well on your way to the Linux adventure. You'll quickly discover all the possibilities offered by this environment, as well as the freedom of customisation it allows. Welcome to the world of Linux!

Conclusion

Acquiring a good knowledge of the Unix/Linux operating system is a major asset for students studying Computer Science with a major in Networks and Maintenance Techniques. This will enable them to stand out in the job market and work on complex IT projects. There are many advantages to learning Unix/Linux, as demonstrated in this book.

In this journey through the intricacies of the Unix operating system and its descendant, Linux, we explore decades development, innovation and challenges. From the birth of Unix in Bell's laboratories to the proliferation of Linux distributions around the world, we have discovered a complex and fascinating universe.

Unix, with its "everything is a file" philosophy and modular architecture, laid the foundations for many modern operating systems. Linux, on the other hand, paved the way for open source and community collaboration. Together, they have shaped computing as we know it today.

But the story doesn't end there. Operating systems continue evolve, adapting to new challenges and meeting the changing needs of users. As we close this book, we know that the adventure continues. New versions, new distributions and new ideas will emerge, driven by a passionate and determined community.

Whether you're a seasoned system administrator, a curious student or simply a computer enthusiast, Unix and Linux will remain faithful companions in your quest for understanding and efficiency. So keep exploring, learning and sharing your knowledge. History is in your hands.

AUTHOR'S DROWNING

The book "Système d'exploitation Unix/Linux" by ***Jeannot FATAKIN. BAZONGA*** offers a complete and in-depth introduction to the use of the free Unix/Linux operating system. It is suitable for beginners who want to learn how to install and manipulate Linux with its graphical interfaces, as well as for more advanced users who want to go further with their computer and test Unix/Linux. This book covers all aspects of Unix/Linux, including comparing Windows and Unix/Linux, installing and configuring Ubuntu, installing free and open-source programs, connecting remotely to a Linux server using SSH and writing Bash scripts. It is easy to understand and gives readers the tools they need to master Linux and start using it for personal or professional purposes.

Printed by Books on Demand GmbH, Norderstedt / Germany